T0324468

Wells Fargo

RALPH MOODY

Illustrated by Victor Mays

UNIVERSITY OF NEBRASKA PRESS
LINCOLN AND LONDON

First Nebraska paperback printing: 2005

Library of Congress Catloging-in-Publication Data
Moody, Ralph, 1898–
Wells Fargo / Ralph Moody; illustrated by Victor Mays.
p. cm.
Originally published: Boston: Houghton Mifflin, 1961.
Includes bibliographical references and index.
ISBN 0-8032-8303-2 (pbk.: alk. paper)
1. Wells, Fargo & Company—Juvenile literature. 2. Brigands and
robbers—United States—Juvenile literature I. Mays, Victor, 1927–
ill. II. Title.
HE5903.W55M66 2005
388.3'41'0978—dc22   2004021029

This Bison Books edition follows the original in beginning chapter 1
on arabic page 11; the text remains unaltered.

CONTENTS

Wells Fargo

I

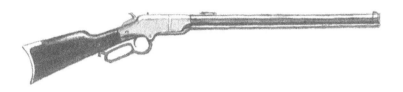

GOLD! GOLD DISCOVERED IN CALIFORNIA! The cry swept through San Francisco like a tornado. It was the spring of 1848. News had just reached the little town of 800 people that James Marshall had discovered a few gold nuggets at Sutter's sawmill in the American River canyon. Half the men in town and half the sailors from ships in the harbor grabbed shovels and gold-washing pans, and rushed for the foothills of the Sierra Nevada Mountains.

Captains of Yankee clippers sped the news around Cape Horn to New York and Boston, while captains of other vessels carried it to every port on the seven seas.

By the spring of 1849 the California gold rush was on in earnest; not only from the eastern United States, but from Mexico, Chile, Australia, China, and a dozen other countries. The early arrivals swarmed like a horde of ants into the canyons of every creek or river that flowed down from the high Sierras. Claims were staked, sand bars ripped into, and at every riffle a dozen gold-crazed prospectors knelt with their washing pans. The strike was fabulous. On some sand bars the gold deposit was so heavy that a man might pan out a thousand dollars' worth of dust in a single day. Claims were divided and redivided, until some were so small they could be covered by a blanket.

California was then a new possession of the United States, ceded by Mexico only the year before, and no written law had yet been established, but, strangely enough, little was needed. In that first great rush every man was so busy panning gold or hunting for it that there was no thought of robbery. A man might sleep soundly with his gold poke on the ground beside him, and have no fear of its being stolen during the night. Alexander Todd, who was California's earliest expressman, was typical of the early stagedrivers. On his first trip from the mining camps to San Francisco he went alone and unarmed, carrying gold dust worth more than $200,000 in a butter keg.

This all changed as the stampede reached its height. The early-comers, the experienced, and the fortunate soon had all the good claims. The late-comers, the inexperienced, the unfortunates, and the shiftless had little or nothing. The more enterprising among the late-comers pushed on deeper into the mountains, and some of them came out with fortunes. The inexperienced usually became discouraged and returned to their homes. The shiftless migrated by thousands to San Francisco, swelling its population from 800 to 25,000 and making it the "wickedest city in the world." But more than a few of the unfortunates stayed in the mountains, and out of bitterness at their misfortunes turned to banditry. By 1851 hardly a day passed without at least one murder being committed, robberies were as common as blackbirds, and no stagecoach carrying gold dust was safe on the highways.

In mid-May Cal Olmstead, driver for the Telegraph Stage Company, climbed to the high seat of his coach in front of the Comptonville Hotel at a few minutes after midnight. At his feet lay a heavy iron express box, fitted with massive bronze hinges, hasp, and padlock. Inside it lay a buckskin sack, filled with gold dust worth $3500, being shipped from mining camps to San Francisco. In the coach six passengers loosened their boots and collars, making themselves as comfortable as possible for the twenty-five-mile ride to Nevada City.

Cal gathered the six reins into one powerful hand, motioned the hostlers who held the rearing lead team to step back, and shouted, "Hiya! Ha! Ha! Ha!" As his long whip writhed above their backs, the three matched pairs of blacks raced down the moonlit street. Without a break in their pace they swung into the first curve on the rutted Nevada City road.

Cal Olmstead was the best driver on the Downieville–Sacramento stage line, and one of the greatest showmen among the famous California jehus, but above all he was a horseman. The touch of his hands on the reins could be as delicate as the fingers of a violinist on his instrument, or as powerful as tempered steel springs. He never drove into a town or out of it with·his horses at less than a high gallop, but on the long stretches of mountain road he nursed their strength as carefully as a mother nurses her child. As soon as the few scattered lights of Comptonville were behind he pulled the blacks down to a steady eight-mile-an-hour trot. On the hard climbs up the steeper hills he walked them, then made up lost time in a breath-taking race down the far side.

For May, the night was chilly. Earlier in the evening it had rained, but now the moon was bright, and the road lay like a carelessly dropped white ribbon as it twisted and wound through the pine- and fir-covered foothills. With skill that seemed almost magic, Cal hurtled the swaying Concord coach down steep canyon walls where the snakelike roadway was scarcely a foot wider than the coach wheels. And ever, above the chuckling of the axle boxes and the pound of racing hoofs, he steadied his horses — and often his frightened passengers — with the calm assurance of his voice: "Ha, Haya, Jack! Steady, Bill! Easy, boy, easy! Haya now! Hi! Hi! Hi!" And from across the canyons the rock walls echoed back the sound of his voice.

The Comptonville stage was due in Nevada City at five o'clock in the morning, but Cal Olmstead was well ahead of time when he crossed the south fork of the Yuba River. He had a full hour left in which to cover the last seven miles, but the 1500-foot climb up the canyon wall was steep, and he wanted his horses fresh enough to make a good fast race into the town.

Cal pulled the blacks to a slow walk, and rested them twice on the long pull up to the canyon rim. He had nearly reached the crown of the last hill north of Nevada City when out of the thicket of chaparral leaped three heavily masked and armed men — a small one in front of the horses, a hulking big fellow covering the passengers in the coach, and a medium-sized leader with his gun aimed at Olmstead's head. "Get down, Cal, and keep your hands up!" he ordered.

Unarmed, Cal Olmstead had no choice but to get down, but he did it with more confidence than might have been expected. The iron express box that held the gold dust was too heavy for the bandits to carry, and too strongly built to be broken open with any tools they might have with them. Beyond this, the leader had called him Cal. Only a local man would have known his name, and only a bungling amateur would have been stupid enough to use it. This, together with their difference in size, should make the bandits easy to catch in case they did get away with the treasure.

It soon became evident to Cal that the bandits, amateurs or not, knew the strength of the iron treasure box and had come well prepared to open it. While Cal was getting down from his high seat, the hulking bandit who had been guarding the passengers ordered them from the coach. He herded them, together with Cal, to the back of the stage, and kept them covered with a pair of cocked six-shooters.

Meanwhile the smallest of the three unhitched the horses, and the leader ducked into the chaparral and brought out a pair of sledge hammers. Together they climbed to the driver's boot of the coach and attacked the iron box furiously. The sound of their hammering rang through the foothills like the clanging of an angry bell, but the box was too stoutly built for their sledges. After a few minutes of useless pounding, the leader straightened up and ordered, "George, fetch me that there can of gunpowder and them fuses!"

The little highwayman scuttled back into the brush, brought out a black can, and scrambled onto the coach again. For several minutes the two knelt over the iron express box. The yellow light of a match flickered for an instant, a fuse sputtered, and the bandits leaped to the ground and ran. They were barely among the chaparral bushes when an explosion rocked the coach. The driver's seat leaped high into the air, sheets of black leather from the boot sailed away like buzzards, but the iron box was unharmed.

When the bandit leader discovered that his carefully laid plan had failed he completely lost his temper and his head. Screaming like a spoiled child, he yelled, "George, fetch me the rest o' that there powder and some heavy rocks! Bob, you keep them passengers covered and let 'em have it if ary one of 'em dasts to move! I'll get this here dust if I have to blow the whole dadburned coach into the bottom of Yuba Canyon!" In desperation he poured all the remaining powder around the great bronze padlock, covered it with stones, lighted the fuse, and leaped for safety.

The explosion crashed with a thunderous roar, the front end of the coach flew apart in splinters, and the iron treasure box plunged to the roadway. Its lock and

hasp were blown to bits, but the buckskin bag of gold dust was undamaged. The bandit leader grabbed it up, tossed it over his shoulder, and raced away into the chaparral, his two henchmen close at his heels.

Steve Vernard, town marshal at Nevada City, was an early riser. His first chore each morning was to clean and oil his most prized possession: one of the few Henry repeating rifles in the California mountains. There were other repeating rifles, but the Henry was the best by far. In a tube mounted beneath the barrel it carried fifteen extra cartridges with half-ounce balls, and each could be flipped into firing position by a back-and-forth swing of the trigger guard. In the hands of an expert the Henry was one of the finest rifles ever designed, and Steve Vernard was an expert. At a hundred yards he could snuff a candle without cutting the wick, and he could fire twenty-five shots in a single minute.

Dawn was just breaking, and Steve Vernard sat cleaning his rifle by the light of a kerosene lamp, when Cal Olmstead slid his galloping horse to a stop at the cabin door. The marshal looked up from the rifle when Cal flung the door open and shouted that he had been robbed, but his hand continued to rub back and forth on the polished barrel. Steve Vernard was no longer a young man, not easily excited, and slow in his movements — except when firing a rifle. "Sit down, son," he said quietly, "and tell it to me again, right from the start. Ain't no sense a-runnin' off into the brush till a man knows what kind of varmints he's after."

Steve kept on with his labor of love as he listened — checking the action of the trigger, the trigger guard, and carefully examining each cartridge in the reloading tube. When Cal had told every detail of the holdup, the marshal looked up and said, "Now ain't that curious? The big one was Bob and the little one George, you say? And the middle-sized one knowed your name? Knowed what the express box was like, too, or he wouldn't have fetched along sledges and gunpowder. Reckon he must have worked for the stage company — or maybe at the hotel up to Comptonville.

"Hmmmmm, hmmmmm . . . Well, I'll be dogged! There ain't no two ways about it; that has to be Jack Williams. Him and Bob Finn and George Moore has been cronyin' abouts for a month or two, but I didn't calculate they had nerve enough betwixt 'em to pull off a stage holdup. Figured 'em for sneak thieves, pickpockets, or the likes. I wouldn't doubt me they'll head down Yuba Canyon towards Marysville. You go on back and look after your passengers whilst I round up a posse."

With a posse of five volunteers, Steve Vernard led the way straight down the steep mountainside into South Yuba Canyon. It would be a waste of time to try finding and following tracks on the rocky ground at the scene of the holdup. If his guess was right, Williams and his henchmen would make a run in the easiest direction: downhill to the bottom of the canyon, then along the south fork westward to the main stream of the Yuba. And, with the rain of the night before, they'd be sure to leave tracks in the damp earth on the lower mountainside.

Near the bottom of the canyon Steve Vernard scattered his posse to hunt for footprints, but it was he who found them. As he expected, they were angling westward, not far up the mountainside from the river. He had followed the tracks less than a hundred yards when they suddenly changed direction to the north, and lengthened. To Vernard the message left by those tracks was as clear as if it had been typed. The amateur highwaymen had discovered they were being followed and, in panic, had raced for the river, where their feet would leave no tracks on the clean-washed granite. If he stopped to gather his posse he could easily lose the thieves among the great boulders that lined the bottom of the canyon. Without hesitation Steve Vernard went on alone.

For a single man to follow three well-armed and desperate criminals into such wild country would seem foolhardy. Knowing they were being followed they could easily ambush him and kill him before he had a chance to raise his rifle. But Steve Vernard wasn't foolhardy. He knew the kind of "varmints" he was following, and he knew how they would behave. That sort of cowards would never risk ambushing one member of a posse and having to fight it out with the others. They'd run for cover, hide out, and fight back only if they were cornered.

Straight across the South Yuba from the point where the thieves had changed direction, Myer's Ravine split the north wall of the canyon like the scar of a mighty cleaver. Its granite walls rose sheer for a hundred feet or more on either side, and its steep, solid-rock floor was strewn with boulders half the size of a cabin. Few better hiding places could be found on earth, and Steve Vernard was positive that Williams and his frightened men were heading for it. He no longer bothered with following their tracks, but cut straight for the mouth of Myer's Ravine.

From melting snowbanks at its head and runoff from the rain of the night before, Myer's Creek was in angry flood. Its roar was deafening as it leaped over boulders in shouting cascades and lashed at its granite walls. A rain of flying spray soaked Vernard to the skin as he climbed cautiously upward, balancing himself with one hand, and holding his rifle safe with the other. Alert for the slightest movement among the boulders, lodged tree trunks, and flying water above him, he

watched for the occasional scratch of a hobnail on stone that told him his quarry was still ahead.

Far up the ravine a granite island stood like a mighty fortress in the center of Myer's Creek. The divided waters cascaded around it, rejoined in a tempest of flying spray, and leaped downward in a fifteen-foot waterfall. Clinging to the rock with feet, knees, and one hand, Steve Vernard inched his way upward to the top of the falls. There a great log was wedged from canyon wall to island, forming a natural bridge. There were no hobnail scratches on the rocks beyond it.

First stopping to check and cock his rifle, Vernard edged cautiously across the wet, slippery bridge. As he stepped off the log and past a shoulder of stone he came face to face with Jack Williams, leveling a cocked .44 revolver unsteadily at him. Beyond Williams and above him, Vernard glimpsed Bob Finn, raising another .44 to take aim. Steve Vernard fired his first shot before he'd brought his rifle fully to his shoulder. He fired the second before the echo of the first could bounce back from the canyon walls. The first made a bull's-eye of Jack Williams's heart; the second caught Bob Finn just above the right eye. He fell with the buckskin bag of gold dust at his feet.

George Moore had not crossed to the island, but in his fright was trying to scale the wall of the canyon as if he were a fly. Vernard sent a warning shot into the wall above him, but Moore stopped only long enough to fire two wild shots toward the island. Steve Vernard's second shot was no warning; Moore's body pitched down the canyon wall into the creek below.

The stage was robbed shortly after four-thirty in the morning. At two o'clock in the afternoon Steve Vernard brought the buckskin bag of gold dust into the Telegraph Stage Company's Nevada City office.

Jack Williams and his followers were fairly representative of California's earliest highwaymen. Most of them were bungling amateurs, men who had been failures all their lives, and no match for a marshal such as Steve Vernard. But there were few Steve Vernards. And bunglers though the early highway-men were, more often than not they were successful in making their robberies and their getaways. The prospectors who struck it rich at the diggings found themselves caught in a dilemma. If they kept their gold dust at their claims they were constantly in danger of being murdered and robbed. If they were lucky enough to get their dust to a stagecoach office and ship it to a San Francisco bank, their chance of losing it to a highwayman was nearly one in four.

Worse still, the early amateurs were soon to be followed by such famous professionals as Rattlesnake Dick, King of the California Highwaymen; Fighting Tom Bell, whose gang of cutthroats terrorized the entire gold region; and Black Bart, the untrackable phantom stage-robber that no marshal or sheriff could run down.

There were only two men in the United States who could successfully solve the gold miners' dilemma: Henry Wells and William Fargo. But until 1852 Wells and Fargo had all they could do to take care of their rapidly growing express business in the East.

Henry Wells and Alvin Adams had been the most successful of the pioneer expressmen in the United States. Both had gone into the business when they were scarcely more than boys, and they had both started from scratch, carrying valuable letters and packages in carpetbags and delivering them for a

Henry Wells

small fee. And, from their earliest years, there had been a keen rivalry between them. Alvin Adams had formed the Adams Express Company, and expanded his business to all the larger cities along the East Coast. By the time gold was discovered in California the Adams firm was the largest express company in the world, and immediately opened a banking and express office in San Francisco.

While Adams built his business in the big cities along the coast, Henry Wells was expanding westward along the Erie Canal. Wells was still a young man when he gained national attention by forcing the United States government to reduce its unreasonably high postage rates. When the Post Office De-

William Fargo

partment was established the mail rate was set at twelve and a half cents for carrying a one-page letter a hundred miles. If there were two pages the rate was doubled, and it was made a finable offense for anyone except a postal employee to carry ordinary mail. Beyond this, the mail service to any point west of Albany was deathly slow and undependable.

Henry Wells could not believe that the government had any right to monopolize a business such as the mail service, and through that monopoly rob its citizens — for certainly the postal rates were nothing short of robbery. A hundred two-page letters would weigh no more than five pounds. To charge twenty-five dollars for carrying so small a weight a hundred miles was outrageous. Furthermore, the law did not make the carrying of mail by others than postal employees a *crime;* it was at worst a finable offense. After careful thought, Henry Wells advertised that his messengers would carry letters between Albany and Buffalo, regardless of the number of pages, for a flat rate of six cents. Within a few weeks Wells's messengers were carrying hundreds of letters on the Albany–Buffalo route to the government's dozens.

The postal authorities could not ignore this threat to the government's monopoly. If Wells were allowed to continue, other expressmen would follow his lead, and the postal monopoly would be ruined. Agents were posted to arrest his messengers whenever they stepped off a stagecoach. To avoid these arrests Wells sent for William Fargo, an excellent horseman and his most resourceful messenger. He told Fargo to buy the fastest horses he could find, mount the letter carriers, and get the mail through in the fastest time he could possibly make.

The affair turned into the greatest fox-and-hound chase the country had ever seen. All along the Erie Canal, Fargo and his riders raced with the forbidden mailbags. Riding by back roads and paths through the woods, they dashed into the little towns, dropped off a few letters, picked up a few more, and raced on. Behind pounded the government agents, with the people along the line throwing them off the trail whenever possible. When, at last, the government had rounded up enough victims and brought them to trial, a local jury found them "Not Guilty!"

The Post Office Department was almost at its wit's end. Other express companies were already following Wells's lead, and this flouting of postal regulations must be stopped immediately. In desperation the Postmaster-General considered taking over all the express companies in the country. Then Henry Wells threw a curve that neither the Postmaster-General nor the Congress could duck. He offered to take over the postal service for the entire country at his company's low rates. Public opinion forced Congress to take action. In 1845 it passed a bill reducing the postage on one-ounce letters to five cents for the first 300 miles, and to ten cents for any point in the country except the Pacific Coast.

During the fight with the Post Office Department Henry Wells recognized in William Fargo the man he wanted for his partner. Together they formed the Western Express Company and expanded their business westward. There was then no railroad west of Buffalo, and all traveling had to be done on river boats, stagecoaches, and horseback, but Wells and Fargo didn't let that worry them. They reached out for all the business there was in the rapidly growing West, opening offices in Cincinnati, St. Louis, and Chicago, and appointing agents in the smaller cities along their routes. By 1850 they had gained complete control of all the express business west of the Allegheny Mountains. That year they joined forces with John Butterfield, another pioneer in this field, and formed the great American Express Company.

The headquarters of the American Express Company were at 16 Wall Street in New York City. Just down the street was the office of the Adams Express Company. Through the winter of 1851–52 Henry Wells and William Fargo watched heavily guarded leathern bags coming into the Adams office whenever ships arrived in the harbor from San Francisco. They needed no one to tell them that these were shipments of gold from the great California bonanza.

This, together with tales that were reaching the East of express holdups in the Sierras, convinced them that their services were not only needed in California but would be profitable there. In the Indian-infested country west of the Alleghenies they had been successful against raids and highwaymen; they'd risk it in California. If John Butterfield thought the western operation would be unwise, they'd form their own company and do it themselves.

The Birth of Wells, Fargo & Company

2

ON MAY 18, 1852, at the Astor House in New York City, the firm of Wells, Fargo & Company was organized. Two days later this announcement was made in the *New York Times:*

WELLS, FARGO & CO.
CALIFORNIA EXPRESS

This company having completed its organisation as above is now ready to undertake the general forwarding agency and commission business; the purchase and sale of gold dust, bullion and specie; also packages, parcels and freight of all description in and between the City of New York and the City of San Francisco, and the principal cities and towns in California.

Samuel P. Carter for many years connected with the American Express, and R. W. Washburn, late of the bank of Syracuse, have been appointed principal agents in California.

The announcement showed clearly that the new

firm would not limit its business to the carrying of valuables. It would carry anything the shipper might want delivered and, furthermore, it would enter the banking business.

The firm of Wells, Fargo & Company was no sooner organized than Carter and Washburn were started for San Francisco. Right behind them went Henry Wells. He wasted no time in San Francisco, but sailed a hundred miles up the river to Sacramento, and there took a stagecoach into the Sierra Nevada Mountains. During the next month he visited as many of the mining camps as possible, studying the needs of the miners and estimating the risk that would be run in handling and transporting gold.

Before Wells had traveled far into the mountains he was convinced that the risk in California would be far greater than he had imagined. At the outset Wells, Fargo & Company would have no stagecoaches of its own. Until they could be bought from the other owners on the coast or brought by sailing ships around South America, Wells Fargo treasure boxes would have to be carried by coaches of the various small stage lines already in operation.

Wells knew from past experience that this would be very risky. There was as yet little law in California, and few sheriffs to enforce what little there was. A stagecoach could travel hardly a mile through the rough mountain country without being at the mercy of any highwayman who took a notion to hold it up. No stagedriver working for another company could be expected to risk his life in protecting a Wells Fargo treasure box. The amount which would be carried in many of the boxes would not justify the expense of sending along a special guard.

Beyond this, there would be passengers on most of the stagecoaches that carried a treasure box. The lives of these passengers would be in danger if there were any shooting in an attempt to resist a robbery. For this reason little resistance could be made. The best policy would be to let the highwaymen take the treasure, then hope to run them down where passengers' lives would not be endangered. Under such circumstances the losses could not help but be great, but the amount of gold to be taken out of those mountains was enormous. Large though the losses might be, Henry Wells believed that with care they could be held to less than 1 per cent of the amount carried.

From Wells's talks with successful miners all through the Mother Lode country, he discovered that their greatest need was to get rid of their gold quickly and safely as soon as it was out of the ground. Although murders were being committed at the rate of more than one a day, a man with an empty gold poke was reasonably safe. But one who was known to have a full poke was in danger of his life at every minute of the day or night. Gold in a miner's poke was of doubtful value; he would gladly pay a fair price to have it safeguarded or delivered without loss to San Francisco or to his family in the East. The miners' greatest complaint was against the government's mail service. The postal rates were excessively high, post offices were widely scattered, and no attempt was made to find those to whom letters were addressed.

By the time Henry Wells had completed his trip to the mining camps, he had determined in his own mind the policies which the new company would follow. First among these would be to provide the greatest possible safety for all honest people concerned, to discourage banditry by making it both dangerous and unprofitable, and to charge rates as low as the risk involved would justify.

In July, 1852, the San Francisco office of Wells, Fargo & Company was opened, and Henry Wells laid down the rules under which the firm would operate: The company would accept no responsibility which it was not financially able to discharge in full. And no customer should ever lose so much as one penny through having entrusted his goods or valuables to the care of Wells Fargo. The firm would make good every loss, regardless of its amount or the circumstances under which it was lost.

Stagedrivers were not to resist a holdup, regardless of the value of treasure being carried, if such resistance would endanger either their lives or the lives of the passengers. Guards would resist holdups at the risk of their own lives, but not at the risk of passengers' lives. Whenever goods or treasure in the care of Wells Fargo were stolen the thieves would be run down and punished, without regard to the time required or the cost involved.

Burglarproof banks would be built at the larger mining towns as rapidly as safes, steel doors, cast-iron shutters, and other building materials could be brought by sailing ships from the East. In all the smaller towns and camps agents would be stationed and offices opened. These banks and offices would be kept open seven days a week, so that miners might quickly dispose of their gold dust near their own diggings, in small amounts and often.

The company would buy gold dust at any of its banks or offices, paying 10 per cent less than the price per ounce being offered at the United States Mint in Philadelphia. Payment would be made in Wells Fargo receipts, which would be redeemed in U.S. currency at either San Francisco or New York.

Miners who wished to do so might turn their gold dust over to any of the Wells Fargo banks or offices for safekeeping. They would seal their dust in buckskin pouches marked with their names, the date, and the weight of gold in each pouch. This gold would remain the private property of the depositor even though the company should fail and declare bankruptcy. Wells Fargo would be responsible for its value if lost by fire, theft, or any other cause, and might not lend the gold for interest or use it in any way whatsoever. The charge for safekeeping of gold would be 1 per cent per month.

Miners wishing to make general deposits of gold dust would be charged only one-half of 1 per cent per month on the balance of their accounts. For each general deposit the miner would be given a Wells Fargo receipt which would be redeemable in gold dust at any time at any bank or office of the company in the mountains. An additional 5 per cent would be charged if the receipts were redeemed at San Francisco, or 10 per cent if redeemed at New York City. Gold dust turned over to the company on general deposit would not remain the private property of the depositor. It might be used by Wells Fargo in any manner it chose, and would become a part of the firm's general assets in case the company should fail.

Wells Fargo mail service would be established at each of the company's banks and offices. Miners already in the camps, or arriving, might register their names and the location of their claims with the agent. The company would keep a record of these names and locations at its home office. Mail arriving at San Francisco for any registered man would be promptly delivered to the office or bank nearest his camp. The charge for handling letters would be one bit (twelve and a half cents); for handling packages which did not contain highly valuable goods the charge would be sixty cents per pound.

The rate for general freight being shipped between New York City and San Francisco would be forty cents per hundred pounds.

The last two provisions of these rules are a fine example of Henry Wells's keen business judgment.

Few men when joining the gold rush had any idea as to what their address might be after reaching California. They knew only that they would get to San Francisco as quickly as possible, then try to find gold somewhere in the mountains. Many of the less fortunate drifted from gulch to gulch and canyon to canyon, panning a few ounces of gold here and a few there, but always moving on in search of a richer strike. Even the most fortunate, those who were able to stake a rich claim, could hardly hope to send word of it to their families in the East and receive a reply within six months. The result was that thousands upon thousands of letters were received at the San Francisco Post Office each month, addressed only to Mr. William Jones, At the Diggings, or Mr. Hiram Smith, San Francisco. While homesick William and Hiram, in some lonely little gulch far back in the mountains, worried about their "folks back home," their letters

were added to the ever-growing mountain of unclaimed mail in San Francisco.

When Henry Wells had made his trip through the
mining camps he had been quick in discovering that
letters from home meant more to many of the miners
than gold itself. He realized fully that twelve and a
half cents a letter would probably not cover the cost
of registering a hundred thousand miners, sorting the
mountain of unclaimed mail at San Francisco, and delivering letters to camps where those to whom they
were addressed were presently to be found. But his

farseeing judgment told him this would be good business, regardless of its cost. From every gulch and canyon in the Mother Lode — California's gold-producing region — men would be coming to Wells Fargo banks and offices to register their names, and they would return often to inquire for mail. The chances were great that they would sell or deposit their gold dust where they came to look for their mail.

The Adams Express Company had joined the gold rush of 1849. By 1852, when Henry Wells made his visit to the mining camps, it was firmly established and doing an enormously profitable business. Its San Francisco bank and office occupied the finest building in the city. Its Concord stagecoaches rolled along every passable road between San Francisco and the Sierra Nevada. Its agents were scattered for two hundred and fifty miles along the Mother Lode. Nearly half of the gold put aboard ship at San Francisco passed through the Adams & Company bank, and most of the freight carried between New York and San Francisco was covered by an Adams waybill.

With a strangle hold on the freight, passenger, and express business, the Adams Express Company set whatever rates it wished on transportation. Together with its friendly competitor, Page, Bacon & Company, it set the price to be paid the miners for their gold dust — and it set that price at a figure that allowed for a generous profit to Adams & Company. The

Adams charge for freight to or from New York City was sixty cents per hundred pounds. Wells Fargo's price of forty cents per hundred, was more than a warning to Adams & Company that its monopoly was ended; it was a bid for the friendship of every San Francisco merchant — and it was a successful bid.

To establish an express, banking, and freight-forwarding business in a new and undeveloped state that was in the throes of a gold rush was neither an easy nor an inexpensive undertaking. Most of the materials for building banks and offices, as well as the workmen who would do the building, had to be brought around Cape Horn from the East. Contracts had to be made with shipowners for transporting Wells Fargo freight, and with the owners of scores of small stage lines for the carrying of express boxes.

San Francisco was overflowing with the riffraff of the world, but honest and ambitious men who could be trusted as agents, bank tellers, clerks, and book-keepers were almost impossible to find. Those strong enough to stand the hard life at the diggings would not quit the search for gold to take such a job. And those honest men who were not strong enough for mining were already employed by the well-established merchants and bankers in San Francisco or Sacramento.

Henry Wells had returned to New York as soon as the policies of the new firm were established. There,

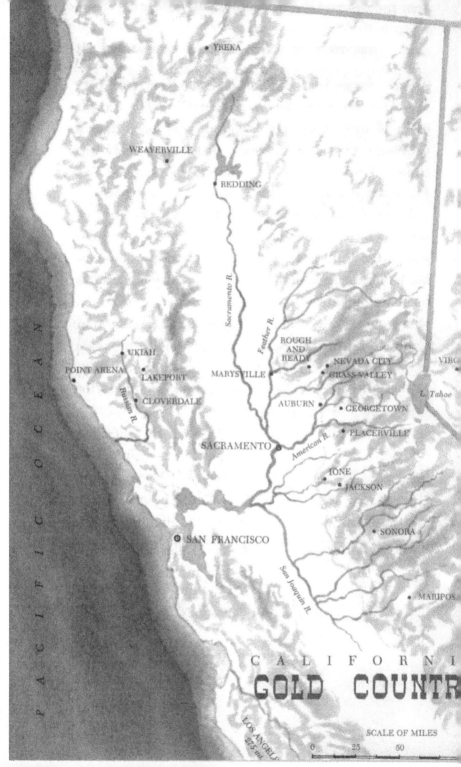

with the help of William Fargo and his other associ-
ates, he set about gathering the materials and skilled
mechanics necessary for the tremendous building
program. As rapidly as the men and materials could
be secured they were loaded into fast Yankee clippers, or steamers, and started on the three-months
voyage around Cape Horn.

Meanwhile in California Samuel Carter and Reuben
Washburn were equally busy. During the summer of
1852 seldom a day passed without some vessel arriving in San Francisco Bay with a horde of fortune
seekers. Reuben Washburn was at the docks to meet
each one of them. Painstakingly he searched through
the newly arrived passengers for those who would
make trustworthy and able employees for Wells Fargo.
His task was to find and train not only agents, gold
buyers, and bookkeepers, but also clerks capable of
handling the toughest assignment on earth — one at
which the United States government had failed completely.

As Washburn hunted out and trained the employees
for the new firm, Sam Carter laid the foundation for
its operation in San Francisco, Sacramento, and the
mining towns and camps of the Mother Lode. A three-
story building was erected at the corner of Montgomery and California streets as the San Francisco
headquarters of the company. Land was bought and
plans made for the building of fort-like brick or stone

banks in the larger mining towns, and for stoutly built log or timber offices in the smaller towns and camps.

Although Adams & Company owned and operated a great fleet of stagecoaches in California, there were dozens of independent stage operators. Many of them had no more than one to four coaches, and most of them did at least a part of their own driving. Often when a ship docked at Sacramento there would be as many as a hundred stagecoaches waiting to rush the gold-crazed passengers to the already overcrowded diggings. Sam Carter rode with every one of these independent coach owners, and seldom left one of them without having made arrangements for the carrying of Wells Fargo treasure boxes. And as he traveled from camp to camp he made friends and kept a sharp lookout for late-comers with courage and honesty who, though unsuccessful as prospectors, would make ideal express guards and messengers.

When Sam Carter was not away in the mountains he was busy in San Francisco or Sacramento: making friends with the merchants, arranging contracts with shipowners, negotiating for the purchase of stage lines, or rounding up freight haulers. Hundreds of them would be needed as soon as ships from the East began arriving with cargoes of materials for Wells Fargo's new banks and offices.

With the coming of fall, vessel after vessel sailed in through the Golden Gate, docked at

San Francisco, or a hundred miles up the river at Sacramento, and discharged its carefully gathered cargo. One after another straining six- and eight-horse teams dragged creaking wagons up the steep, rugged roads to the towns and camps of the Sierra Nevada — one loaded with the ponderous steel doors for the Wells Fargo bank at Big Oak Flats, another with the cast-iron window shutters for Marysville, and a third with brick for the bank at Placerville. Half-way up Carson Hill a sixteen-horse hitch stood blowing and catching its wind. On the massive-wheeled freight schooner behind it rode the burglarproof and fireproof safe for the already half-built bank at Sonora.

At the headquarters building of the company in San Francisco a score of highly skilled steelworkers, sent by the manufacturer in the East, were installing the great treasure vaults. Inch-thick steel plates were being riveted into place, while masons laid up yard-thick surrounding walls to protect the vaults from fire. At the golden-oak counter that stretched the full length of the main banking room, silk-hatted gold buyers stood behind brightly polished brass scales, so finely balanced that they would indicate 1/100th of an ounce. Dozens of well-trained postal clerks were listing the names of miners who had registered at the camps, and sorting the mountain of unclaimed mail from the U.S. Post Office in San Francisco. Safety

and service were to be the watchwords of Wells Fargo, and no expense was being spared to insure them.

Along with the other materials and equipment shipped from the East were scores of Wells Fargo mailboxes. They were about a foot square by six inches deep, with a slanting top that extended well out over the front and sides like a roof. With their bright green paint and round peephole in the front, they looked more like little birdhouses than mailboxes. Soon there was a little green box bolted securely to a post in front of every hotel and at most of the street corners in San Francisco and Sacramento, and letters were dropped into them in ever-increasing numbers.

By this time no ship docked in San Francisco without bringing passengers who had come to join friends or relatives already in the mining camps. Few of these newcomers had any idea that there were hundreds of different camps scattered through the Sierra Nevada for a distance greater than that between Boston and Philadelphia. Many of them knew only that the man for whom they were looking was somewhere at the diggings. It was not uncommon for a new arrival to hurry down the gangplank and ask the first old-timer he saw, "Can you tell me how to get to the new diggin's? I'm looking to find Lance Phillips there."

"Which new diggin's?"

"Is there more than one?" the newcomer would ask.

"Lance, he's my brother. I got a letter from him last spring, postmarked at San Francisco and sayin' he'd struck it rich in the new diggin's."

"That don't mean nothin'," the old-timer would tell him. "There ain't a day goes by that there ain't a new diggin's somewheres, and one that was new a year agone is like as not a ghost camp 'fore now. A man might as leave hunt for one perticular flea on a dog as for one perticular man in them mountings. I'll tell you what you do, stranger: You see that little green box over yonder? Well, you write a letter to your brother, telling him whereat you'll be stoppin' here in the city, and drop it in that box. Them Wells Fargo folks, they'll find him if he's still alive and kickin', and 'twon't be more'n a week or two 'fore you'll hear from him."

If the newcomer followed the old-timer's advice, he usually found his brother, and Wells Fargo found two new friends.

Until snow clogged the mountain roads solidly, the great freight wagons, loaded with Wells Fargo materials, rolled between the docks and the mining camps. But neither snow nor sub-zero weather stopped the hundreds of carpenters, masons, steelworkers, and loggers who were building the banks and offices. By the end of 1852 there were Wells Fargo offices open in mining camps all along the Mother Lode. Most of them were built of logs or heavy planking. In each there was a fireproof steel safe, and an agent was on duty to buy gold, receive deposits, accept dust pokes for safekeeping, and handle mail.

On the main street of each of the larger mining towns the new bank building stood out like a fortress. The thick side and back walls were usually built from rough slabs of hand-split mountain stone, but the fronts were often fine examples of the fanciest brick work of the period. At each window hung a pair of heavy cast-iron shutters, made in Brooklyn, New York, and always painted bright green. The wide doors were made from two plates of half-inch steel, hung on ponderous hinges and stoutly barred at the center. Above them, or on a canopy that extended over the sidewalk, was the bright green sign with gold lettering: WELLS, FARGO & CO. EXPRESS.

The room inside was divided into three sections, the one at the back being cut off by a stone wall to form the vault, or, as it was called, the treasure room. These walls were so massive that nothing less than a great charge of dynamite would break them, and the steel door that closed the only opening often weighed more than a ton.

The front section was surrounded by benches for customers, and for passengers who might be waiting for stagecoaches. Behind this, and stretching from wall to wall, was a solidly built counter of golden oak. At one end was the post office, where miners lined up to look for letters whenever a stage came in. At the other end was the package and baggage department. At the center of the counter gold buyers and tellers stood behind their brightly polished scales, while bearded miners jostled one another, each anxious to have his dust weighed first. Leaning against the counter or circulating among the miners was a tight-lipped guard or two, eyes watching for the first suspicious movement, a .45 Colt slung at his belt and a sawed-off shotgun across his arm.

3

IT IS almost impossible for any man or any firm to make a great many friends without also making a few enemies. Wells Fargo was no exception, and the enemies it made were powerful.

Before Wells Fargo entered the California express and banking business, the Adams Express Company had owned more stagecoaches than all its rivals combined, handled most of the gold dust shipped down from the mountains, and divided the banking and gold-buying business with Page, Bacon & Company. The profits of these two great companies were enormous, and they had no intention of letting them be cut by this new competitor who had swept into their territory like a whirlwind. Together they determined to bankrupt Wells Fargo and drive it out of business, even though they had to forego any further profits until their purpose was accomplished.

As soon as Wells Fargo opened its doors, Page, Bacon & Company and Adams & Company raised the price offered for gold dust. Since Page, Bacon &

Company had no stagecoach or express business, Adams & Company made their greatest fight against Wells Fargo on the highways and in the mining towns. If the new outfit thought it could win the friendship of miners by giving them fast mail service, Adams & Company would give them still faster service. If Wells Fargo thought it could muscle in on the express business, Adams & Company would buy out all the independent stage lines and cut off every way for the new firm to get its treasure boxes carried.

For more than two years the rivalry for control of the banking and express business in California was turned into a dog fight, and Wells Fargo was the underdog. Page, Bacon & Company kept its price for gold dust high, and increased its good will with the San Francisco and Sacramento merchants by making them large loans on small security. Adams & Company bought out one stage line after another, until it had coaches rolling over every road from Los Angeles to Portland, Oregon. It established mail service throughout the entire 20,000 square miles of the Mother Lode and put on special messengers to rush news to the papers in the larger towns.

To meet the competition, Wells Fargo was forced to buy stage lines at outrageous prices and to hire fast pony riders for carrying its mail. Speed became a craze in the express and mail service throughout the whole state. Stagedrivers lashed their galloping six-horse teams around hairpin turns high on the canyon walls. Stagecoaches rocked and pitched like bucking broncos, while passengers clung to their seats with both hands, and skidding wheels flung rocks into the gorges below. Relays of pony riders whipped their mounts along trails that would have frightened a mountain goat, racing to beat their rivals through to the mining towns with the latest news for the papers.

Both Wells Fargo and Adams & Company often spent thousands of dollars on a single race where the postage charged was no more than a few cents. And still more thousands were bet by the miners and townspeople on the outcome of the races. Both companies kept messengers and fast horses waiting at San Francisco and upriver at Sacramento to meet ships arriving with mail and news from the East. Within minutes after a ship docked the messengers would claim the mail and newspapers sent in care of their companies, and the race for the mountains would be on.

In the fall of 1853 President Pierce delivered an important message to Congress, and a copy of it was expected to reach San Francisco by steamer in December. At that time the fight between Wells Fargo and Adams was at its height. Both companies had recently extended their services to Portland, and both were anxious to beat the other there with a copy of the President's message. It was known that the Portland newspapers would give a great deal of pub-

licity to the express company which was first to reach them with the news, and both firms wanted that free advertising. Each tried to keep its preparations for the race a secret from the other, but each firm sent agents to hire the fastest horses and riders that could be found between the two cities. The distance was more than six hundred miles. Every ten miles along the route Wells Fargo had a keeper and a fast horse stationed. The keepers were ordered to have their horses grained, saddled, and ready to go at any moment from December 28 until the relay rider should arrive.

It was January 3 when the steamer carrying New York newspapers which contained President Pierce's message arrived. The race that followed was one of the greatest that ever took place in California. In telling of it, Bill Lowden, who carried the Adams mailbag between Tehema and Weaverville, said: "The race was very close from San Francisco to Tehema. Wells Fargo led at Marysville. Between Marysville and Tehema, Adams & Co.'s messenger passed Wells Fargo's rider, and reached the river first and crossed to the Tehema side just as Wells Fargo's man reached the opposite bank.

"Here my race commenced. I sprang into the saddle with the bags, which weighed 54 pounds. I changed horses nineteen times between Tehema and Shasta, touching the ground but once. This was at the Prairie House, where Tom Flynn, the man in charge of my horse, was actively engaged in a fight with the keeper of Wells Fargo's horse and had let mine get loose. I rode my tired horse a little past where the fight was going on, sprang to the ground, caught a fresh horse by the tail and went into the saddle over his rump at a single bound. Turning to the horse I had just left with the express bags, I pulled them over on my fresh horse and renewed the race. I lost about one minute here.

"All other changes I made while the horses were running, the keeper leading the horse I was to ride and riding his extra horse. I would make myself heard with a whistle about half a mile before reaching the change, which gave ample time to tighten the cinch and start the fresh horse on the road. When I reached him, the keeper would have my horse in a lively gallop, and I sprang from the one to the other. . . .

"I reached Shasta, sixty miles, in two hours and thirty-seven minutes . . . I had nine changes of horses between Shasta and Weaverville (the last five being owned by me and hired by Adams for the race), and reached the latter place in five hours and thirteen minutes from the time I left Tehema. From Shasta to Weaverville was run after dark, with a light snow falling, but when I had my favorite horses to ride snow did not make much difference in speed. My stock and help for this race cost Adams & Co. about $2,000."

The total amount received by Adams and Wells Fargo for mail and express carried on this ride could not have brought the two companies more than forty dollars, but they had each spent more than ten thousand in an effort to beat the other. In this particular race Adams & Company won, but if records had been kept of all the races between riders and drivers of the two companies, honors would have been about even.

On June 2, 1854, the San Francisco *Alta California* reported: "A few moments after the arrival of the Sacramento boat last evening, the wagons of Adams and Wells Fargo expresses came dashing down Mont-gomery Street at full speed, Wells Fargo about three lengths ahead, throwing with considerable accuracy the up-river exchanges into the door of our office."

Besides furnishing entertainment for the miners and townspeople, the greatest effect of this rivalry was a vast improvement of the mail service throughout the state. The United States government's postal service in California had been slipshod and undependable from the beginning, but the postage rates were more than double those charged in the East. As the service of the express companies improved, the people stopped using the United States mail almost entirely.

Daniel Haskell, California partner of Adams & Company, gloated over the amount of mail his firm had been able to take away from Wells Fargo and the government. And Daniel Haskell was no man to hide his light under a bushel. Late in 1853 he issued postage stamps for mail to be carried over Adams & Company's lines, and could think of no more appropriate face to appear on these stamps than his own. It is believed that they were the only express or private postage stamps ever issued in the United States bearing the likeness of their issuer.

Until Haskell issued his self-advertising postage stamps the U.S. Post Office Department had raised little objection to the expressmen's carrying of mails in California. But this was a little more than the Postmaster-General would stand for. In January, 1854, he sent an order to San Francisco demanding that mailable material, whether carried by postal employees or express companies, must bear United States government stamps.

Never before or since has there been such bitter criticism of a government department in the United States. Henry Wells believed this to be an unjust and unreasonable order, since it was actually a tax instead of a charge for services. He instructed Wells Fargo officials not to enforce it. The people of California demanded that the government get out of the mail service and leave it in the more skillful hands of the expressmen. The *Alta California,* San Francisco's leading newspaper, ran a scathing editorial:

> The present Post Office system is the most outrageous ever imposed upon a free people. It forbids us from sending letters by such means of conveyance as we may prefer, without paying an odious and onerous tax to the government. A private individual cannot carry letters, because it would interfere with the government monopoly, and so the Post Office charge must be paid, whether the service is rendered by it or not. . . . The Post Office system, so far as California is concerned, is a humbug and a nuisance. It subjects correspondents to an onerous tax if they select a more speedy and sure conveyance for their letters than the mail, and it benefits no one save office holders and contractors. . . . To sum it all up, it is a tyrannical and worse than useless institution and ought to be abolished.

Haskell's stamps had annoyed the Postmaster-General, but editorials such as this infuriated him. He issued a new order, placing a fine of fifty dollars on every piece of mailable material found in the possession of an expressman without U.S. stamps attached. But Wells Fargo still refused to demand government stamps on mail which it handled. Cooler heads in the Post Office Department remembered when another Postmaster-General had tangled with Henry Wells and come off second best. They had no wish for another tangle, so the order was never enforced. Instead, the postal rate in California was slashed to three cents for letters.

Even with the postage reduced to three cents the people of California would not use the undependable government mail service. They preferred to send their letters by Wells Fargo or Adams & Company, and had no objection to the expressmen's charge of 12½¢, but they flatly refused to put government stamps on letters sent by express. Henry Wells now believed that it was the people of California rather than the government who were being unreasonable, but he was too good a businessman to incur their ill will by refusing to handle mail which did not bear government postage. Wells Fargo would pay this small tax if the people were unwilling to. In a single year the company bought more than three million government three-cent envelopes, placed its own mark on them, and sold them to customers for the regular price of one bit. Adams & Company and the few independents still in the express business soon followed suit.

Although Wells Fargo bought out several independent stagecoach and express businesses during the first two years of its operation, it was still far behind its great competitors in the gold-buying and banking

business. The two older companies had plunged head-
long into banking, paying high prices for gold, lend-
ing it freely at high interest rates, and making a large
part of their profits on loans. By following the same
course, Wells Fargo might have greatly increased its
banking business and its profits, but it held fast to
Henry Wells's original principles. No loans were made
unless they were well secured, and when losses oc-
curred — as they often did — they were made good
from the firm's own funds, not from the funds of their
depositors.

After two years of operation Wells Fargo was still
running a poor third to its two great rivals. A steamer
leaving San Francisco Harbor on November 17, 1854,
carried a Page, Bacon & Company shipment of nearly
half a million dollars in gold dust. Adams & Company's shipment was $350,000. But Wells Fargo's was
only $177,000. By that time Adams & Company had
spread its service to cover the whole West Coast, and
had even opened a branch in Australia. Under the
driving fists of Isaiah Woods and Daniel Haskell the
company was growing by leaps and bounds. It looked
as though they might make good their threat to
squeeze out the more conservative Wells Fargo firm.

From 1849 through 1853 the Mother Lode had
poured out its gold in what seemed to be a never-
ending stream. Then as now, few men could stand
sudden prosperity. Many of the prospectors headed

for San Francisco and a gay celebration as soon as they had their pokes full of gold dust. Within a few days they returned to the diggings dead-broke. The merchants, saloonkeepers, owners of gambling houses, and sharpers of every known kind grew fat on the gold the prospectors had flung carelessly away.

A pair of boots or a jacket that cost the merchant no more than three dollars would often be sold to a drunken miner for twenty. There seemed to be no end to the business, and the merchant's biggest problem was to get enough merchandise to keep his shelves full. All of his goods had to be bought for cash in the East, then brought more than 15,000 miles

around Cape Horn by sea. He could not hope to receive them for at least six months after they had been ordered and paid for.

To do business under these circumstances required tremendous amounts of money, for a merchant often had ten or twelve times as much merchandise bought and on shipboard as he had on the shelves of his store. If he found himself short of cash he could always borrow from Page, Bacon & Company or Adams & Company. Their interest rates were unreasonably high, but this didn't worry him. The profit he'd make on goods would also be unreasonably high, so he could well afford the interest. Most of the merchants were greedy. As the gold continued to flow from the mountains they enlarged their stores and doubled the size of the orders they sent east for merchandise. They also doubled the size of their loans from the bankers.

The winter of 1853–54 was mild in the Sierra Nevada. Little snow fell, and in the lower foothills of the mountains the prospectors were able to work their claims all through the winter. The spring was early and warm. The snow on the high range melted rapidly, and the creeks and rivers became rushing torrents, making gold washing along them impossible. Within a few weeks most of the snow was gone. No rain fell during the late spring and hot summer. The creeks and rivers dried up or became mere trickles.

At that time there was almost no hard-rock mining in California. Ninety per cent of the gold was being panned from the sand bars along the streams, or washed from gravel banks by powerful streams of water. With the creeks dried up and the rivers reduced to a trickle, the rich gravel banks could not be worked. Only the fortunate miners whose claims were along the larger river beds had water for their pans and sluice boxes — and without it no gold could be washed from the sand.

Thousands of miners who could not work their claims for lack of water spread out farther to the north, to the south, and higher toward the backbone of the Sierras, hunting for new outcroppings of gold. But the new strikes were few, and none of them rich. Some outcroppings of gold veins were found in hard rock, but hard-rock mining required heavy machinery and stamping mills. The California miners of the early fifties had neither. As, one after another, the disappointed prospectors returned from their search, the frightening word spread through the camps that there might soon be an end to the great bonanza; that the Mother Lode might already have given up the richest part of her treasure.

That summer of 1854 there were few miners in the camps with bulging gold pokes, and still fewer came to the big cities to scatter their dust recklessly. Those who were fortunate enough to have water with which to pan gold held on to their precious dust, or deposited it with Adams & Company or Wells Fargo.

Meanwhile steamers and sailing vessels from the East continued to arrive in San Francisco Bay, loaded to the gunwales with goods that the merchants had ordered and paid for six months before. With the trade from the mining camps reduced to as small a trickle as flowed in the mountain streams, the merchandise on the merchants' shelves piled high. But still the flood of goods poured into San Francisco with every ship that docked. Prices were reduced to less than cost in an effort to get rid of some part of the glut, but there were few or no buyers. Soon every warehouse in the city was filled to the roof with goods

for which there was no market. Boots that had sold the year before at twenty dollars a pair were being offered for two dollars. And still the flood of merchandise poured in. Before cancellations could be sent to the manufacturers in the eastern cities, the goods were already on shipboard and out to sea. The bankers began demanding payment of their past-due loans, but with sales almost at a standstill the merchants could not meet the demands. They had no money with which to build additional warehouses, and with those they had already filled they could do nothing but allow the incoming goods to pile up mountain-high on the docks. And there they were ransacked by thieves.

As early as 1850 San Francisco had been given the reputation of being the wickedest city in the world. During the summer of 1854 it earned that reputation beyond any possible doubt. With the flood of celebrating miners no longer coming in from the mountains, the crooks and sharpers who had preyed upon them turned to thievery, blackmail, and murder. The politics of San Francisco was controlled by thugs, the city government was corrupt, and there was scarcely an honest judge to be found in any of the courts. From the dried-out mining camps, prospectors who had flung their gold away on celebrations came back to San Francisco in search of jobs. But there were no jobs, and men who might otherwise have remained honest turned to thievery and crime when they were at the point of starvation.

To add fuel to the flame, ships began arriving in the late fall with hordes of job seekers from the East. Each of these ships brought word of hard times in the East: of thousands out of work in the cities, of bread lines and bank failures. The headquarters of Page, Bacon & Company at St. Louis called upon its San Francisco branch for an immediate shipment of a million dollars in gold.

The blow that nearly crippled California fell on February 17, 1855. That day the steamer *Oregon* arrived at San Francisco from Panama with news that drafts on the St. Louis office of Page, Bacon & Company had been dishonored in New York City. In other words, Page, Bacon & Company in St. Louis was on the point of failure. And the last steamer to leave San Francisco Bay before the *Oregon* arrived had carried away a million dollars from the firm's San Francisco office.

Some of the San Francisco newspapers tried to prevent a run on Page, Bacon & Company by failing to print the news brought by the *Oregon*, and no mention was made of the million dollars which had been shipped away. But secrets are hard to keep in a city that is already on the verge of panic, and bad news always spreads quickly. On February 18, depositors began withdrawing their money from Page, Bacon &

Company. They would trust it to no other bankers but hid it away in cellars and garrets. By the 22nd the run had become a mad scramble. Page, Bacon & Company paid out what U.S. currency and gold dust it had in its vaults, then closed its doors forever. It still owed its depositors and creditors a million dollars — the exact amount that had been shipped away one day before the news that brought on the crash had been received.

Fear is the mother of panic, and panic is a disease that spreads like wildfire, robbing men of their reason and turning the weaker of them into rioting beasts. The news brought by the *Oregon* frightened the Californians who had their gold dust or money deposited with Page, Bacon & Company. As rumors that the San Francisco branch of that firm was on the verge of failure were whispered about the city, the fear turned into panic. The disease spread quickly to the depositors in every other bank, and they rushed to Montgomery Street — the Wall Street of San Francisco. They stormed the offices of Wells Fargo, Adams & Company, and the smaller private banks along the street, fighting each other for a chance to get in and withdraw their money before these banks too should fail.

The depositors were soon joined by the riffraff of the town. They turned the stampede into a riot, hoping that the bank vaults might be broken into and

that they might be able to get their hands on the plunder. The whole half-mile of Montgomery Street was jammed with a fighting, howling mob.

In 1855 as now, no bank kept all of its depositors' money on hand and ready for immediate withdrawal. The operation of a bank is very expensive, and this expense can be covered only by investing a reasonable part of the deposits. Now each state and the Federal Government enforces strict banking laws which limit

the portion of a bank's deposits that may be invested, and the type of investments that may be made. In 1855 California had no such banking laws, and the Federal Government was far away in Washington. The bankers in this new state did as they pleased with their depositors' money. Those who were greedy for profits loaned as much of it as they dared, and wherever the highest interest could be charged. The more conservative loaned or invested only what they believed to be safe, and were careful in the type of loans they made. Wells Fargo had been conservative; Adams & Company, greedy.

The small and corrupt police force in San Francisco was unable, or unwilling, to control the rioting mob in Montgomery Street, but the buildings occupied by both Adams & Company and Wells Fargo were veritable fortresses. Both firms put shotgun guards at their doors and let in only those who could show by receipts that they were depositors. The rioting had begun in the forenoon of Thursday, Washington's Birthday. All through the day Adams & Company on the west side of Montgomery Street, and Wells Fargo on the east, let customers in and paid off their deposits as fast as the tellers could handle them. By closing time the amount of U.S. currency and gold bullion left in the Adams & Company vaults was far too small to take them through another day.

The telegraph lines between California and the East were not completed until six years after the panic of 1855, but lines had recently been run between San Francisco and the larger cities and towns of central California. As soon as the run on Adams & Company's Montgomery Street office began, Isaiah Woods and Daniel Haskell sent frantic telegrams to their agents in Sacramento, Stockton, Sonora, and other of their larger branches, ordering them to ship large amounts of gold to San Francisco immediately.

The same wires that carried the frantic orders also carried news of the panic in San Francisco, and it rushed like a tornado throughout the state. Even so, it was not fast enough to save many of the Adams depositors. Some of their more favored depositors in the outlying cities and towns were paid off before the vaults were emptied, but many of the less favored got little or nothing. The Adams branch at Sacramento ran out of funds and closed early on Friday morning. At Stockton the sheriff seized all gold coming in on Adams & Company stagecoaches before the agent could get hold of it and ship it on to San Francisco. In Auburn and Sonora, where the sheriffs were not quick enough to catch the gold before it got away, the mobs broke into the Adams & Company vaults and grabbed whatever money was still on hand. Even with the shipments of gold from its branches, the Adams bank in San Francisco could not meet the demands of its depositors and closed its doors on Friday.

With the failure of Adams & Company the rioters in San Francisco went wild. Wells Fargo and a few of the small private banks were still paying off depositors, but it was no longer safe to continue. The panic was entirely out of hand. Shops, stores, and wholesale houses locked their doors and barricaded their windows. Even the courts adjourned. The rioting had spread to Sacramento, and in both cities Wells Fargo hung signs on its doors:

To our Depositors — We have deemed it pru-
dent for the protection of your interests as well
as ours, to close our doors today. We shall make
such a statement of our affairs and abundant
ability to pay as we trust will satisfy all.

WELLS FARGO AND CO.

Feb. 23, 1855

An independent temporary receiver was immediately appointed to examine the accounts of the company, and on the following day he issued this statement:

Wells Fargo & Co. have completed a balance
of their accounts this day, and find to the credit
of their house above every liability $389,106.23,
and only ask of their friends a few days to con-
vert some of their assets to resume payment.

WELLS FARGO & CO.

Saturday, 10 P.M.

That same day Isaiah Woods of Adams & Company,
dressed as a woman, sneaked out of San Francisco and
boarded a fast ship for Australia. But the officers of
Wells Fargo had nothing to run from. Their investments were sound and when, at the first of the week,
they again opened their banks the panic had ended.
Many of those who had been fortunate enough to
withdraw their money from the banks of Page, Bacon

& Company or Adams & Company began digging it out of its hiding places and depositing it with Wells Fargo. Several of the independent banks had weathered the panic and again reopened their doors, but none of them were also engaged in the express business.

The fight had been long and hard, but Wells Fargo had won through by sticking steadfastly to the policies laid down by Henry Wells. It was now in complete control of the express business in California, and by far the West's leading banker. Its express and banking offices stretched from Portland to San Diego.

When Adams & Company failed, its stagecoach lines were seized by its creditors, who operated them for a short time, but they were soon sold to Wells Fargo. Before the end of the decade Wells Fargo stages rolled over every passable road in California, and reached over into Oregon and Nevada. It was soon to become the largest stagecoach operator in the world.

4

GOOD AND BAD fortune often come in waves, and California's fortunes turned upward soon after the panic of 1855 was ended. Rain came in the mountains, allowing the miners to work their claims again. A new gold strike was made in the Kern River country, and the business of the cities again became flourishing.

Even with the return of business, San Francisco remained the wickedest city in the world, and it was steadily growing wickeder. It had become the Mecca for thieves and murderers from every country on earth. With many of the courts, the city government, and the police department controlled by thugs, no honest man dared walk the streets unarmed.

By the spring of 1856 the crime in the city had become so terrible that the honest citizens banded together and formed the famous Vigilance Committee. The criminals were rapidly rounded up and tried for their crimes. The worst of them were hanged, many imprisoned, and thousands driven from the city by fear of punishment. Unfortunately for Wells Fargo, many of the most desperate criminals were driven into the mountains — where there was little or no law, but many Wells Fargo stagecoaches carrying treasure boxes.

Stage holdups had been no novelty in California, but until the Vigilance Committee drove the big-time criminals out of San Francisco, most of the holdups were small and carried out by a single highwayman. The one exception had been the short-lived Reelfoot Williams gang. In 1852 Reelfoot had organized a gang of young toughs, and the smartest among them was Rattlesnake Dick. They held up the Nevada City stagecoach, robbed it of the express box containing $7500, and took off toward the high mountains. The sheriff of Yuba County promptly swore in a posse, picked up the trail of the bandits, and ran them down. Three of the gang were killed, others were captured and jailed, but Reelfoot and Rattlesnake Dick escaped to San Francisco and disappeared into its underworld.

Dick Barter was born in Quebec, the son of a British army officer. At seventeen years of age he ran away from home and joined the California gold rush. He was tall, handsome, smart, and a crack shot with either pistol or rifle. For a short time he prospected unsuccessfully at Rattlesnake Bar, then fell in with a crowd of rough young miners, became their leader, and was given the name Rattlesnake Dick. He had not been leader of the rough crowd long before he was arrested for horse-stealing, was convicted and sent to the penitentiary. Soon after, it was discovered that he was not guilty of the crime. He was released and went to Shasta to make a fresh start, but the name of "Rattlesnake Dick, the horse thief," followed him, and honest people would have nothing to do with him. Embittered and unable to make a living, Dick decided to earn the reputation for thievery that had been unjustly given him. It was soon after that he joined Reelfoot's gang.

The speed with which Williams's gang was run down and broken up taught highwaymen a lesson they did not soon forget: gang robbery was too dangerous. It was much easier for a posse to follow the trail of a gang than of a single man. Then too, if one member of a gang were caught there was always danger that he might "sing to save his neck," and give away the name of every other man in the gang.

On the other hand, it was reasonably safe for a highwayman to make a stickup alone. There were thousands of places along the mountain roads where he could lie in hiding until a stagecoach pulled slowly up a steep, narrow road. There was no chance for the driver to whip his team into a dash for safety. Regardless of how brave and watchful a guard might be, he was always at a disadvantage. On his high seat beside the driver he was a perfect target for a bandit in hiding. Often his first warning of a holdup was the sight of a double-barreled shotgun aimed at his head. Beyond this, there were usually passengers in the stagecoach, and the highwaymen knew that guards were instructed to give up their treasure boxes before endangering the lives of their passengers.

There was no need for more than one man in pulling such a holdup, and — until Wells Fargo established its detective force — his risk of being killed or caught was slight. Often the highwayman himself was never seen by those he robbed. With only his gun barrel showing through a clump of chaparral, he would shout, "Throw down the box!" Nine times out of ten it was thrown down, and as soon as it struck the ground the robber shouted, "Drive on!"

The driver had no choice but to do as he was told. And it took a brave guard to climb down and go back to fight it out alone with the bandit. Well hidden in the brush, a highwayman had been known to follow for a mile or more a stagecoach he had robbed, and to riddle the guard with buckshot at his first move to leave his seat.

With the treasure box in the road and the stagecoach driven beyond rifle range, the robber's task was easy. He had only to smash the lock off the box, lift out the gold pouches and slip away into the chaparral. If he were reasonably careful about leaving tracks, he could no more be trailed through that wilderness of brush-covered hills than a red ant could have been. And if he were smart enough to keep from getting drunk and doing a little bragging, he could soon be spending his plunder freely and without being suspected of his crime. He had only to disappear for a few days, then show up in some mining town with a tall tale of having struck a rich sand bar. Gold dust was gold dust, and stolen dust looked the same as any other. Often a highwayman deposited in a Wells Fargo bank the gold he had stolen from a Wells Fargo treasure box the week before.

Following the breakup of Reelfoot Williams's gang, Rattlesnake Dick remained in the San Francisco underworld for three years. But the panic made robbery unprofitable there, so he went back to look for better picking in the hills. For a short while he held up stagecoaches alone. But he was a natural leader of men, and was soon at the head of the first successful gang of highwaymen in the West. Dick's first big strike, and one that brought him fame, was the $80,000 robbery of a Wells Fargo mule train.

The messenger and guard chosen by Wells Fargo to take this large shipment from the mountains to Shasta City were brave and well experienced. They knew the manner in which lone highwaymen made their holdups, and were careful to guard against it. To move so large a shipment by stagecoach, even though there were no passengers to be protected, would be too risky. It would be much safer to move it by mule train. The gold dust, weighing slightly over three hundred pounds, could be divided between two mules, but they would take eight or ten in the train.

With the messenger at the front of the mule train and the guard at the rear, a highwayman would have little chance. If the messenger were surprised and covered by a shotgun, the guard could slip into the brush and attack the would-be robber from the rear. Or, if the bandit were one of the few treacherous ones who shot without warning, the guard could pick him off before he had a chance to discover which of the mules were carrying the treasure.

As an extra precaution, the messenger chose mules that knew the trail well and were from a corral in

Shasta City. To insure secrecy, they were saddled before dawn in a corral guarded by well-trusted Wells Fargo men. Each pack saddle was exactly alike, and to keep the weights equal the gold was placed in the center of two packs, sand in the center of the others. Then the train of mules was put onto the trail without halters or bridles. This would make them difficult to catch, and if stampeded they would run straight to their home corral, carrying the gold with them.

The April sun bore down unusually hot. The string of sweating mules plodded slowly up the steep trail along a canyon side, their heads low and their ears flopping wearily. At the head of the single file walked

the messenger, and at the rear the guard, each with his shotgun held at the ready and his eyes watching for the slightest movement in the thick brush above the trail. More than half their route had been covered without trouble, but this was the most dangerous spot along the trail. With both men watching the brush sharply, the mules plodded on until the leader had reached the top of the grade.

Suddenly a deep voice from the brush barked, "Holdup!" Both guard and messenger swung instinctively, their shotguns trained in the direction from which the sound had come. Instantly each was challenged from behind, and whirled back to find a shot-

gun leveled at his head from point-blank range. While the luckless Wells Fargo men were being disarmed other bandits leaped into the trail, shouting and stampeding the mules.

As had been expected, the mules returned to their home corral, but when they got there the gold was gone from the packs that had been loaded with the treasure.

As quickly as news of the big holdup could be flashed to San Francisco, Wells Fargo rushed its best detectives to the scene of the robbery. There they found plenty of sign to show there had been as many as a half-dozen bandits in the holdup gang that had ambushed the mule train. But not a single footprint could be found that led away from the spot. The highwaymen had disappeared as tracklessly as if they had been crows. From one end of California to the other Wells Fargo posted notices of the holdup, offering huge rewards for information leading to the arrest of any member of the gang. If anyone outside the gang had such information, he was either too loyal or too much afraid of the consequences to claim the reward. Wells Fargo could only lick its costly wound and wait for the bandit to strike again.

The wait was long. Here and there throughout the 20,000 square miles of the Mother Lode, lone highwaymen held up stages and robbed them of their treasure boxes. On these the newly organized Wells Fargo detective force sharpened its wits as the summer and fall of 1855 passed. A few of the highwaymen made complete getaways, but two thirds of them were run down, the treasure recovered, and the robbers sent to jail. But no trace of the mule-train robbers had ever been found, nor had they struck again.

Then, early in 1856, a Rhodes and Lusk Express messenger was held up and robbed of $26,000. It was a gang holdup, and there was no question but that it had been pulled by the mule-train gang. The holdup was excellently planned, carried out with the precision of clockwork, and no trail was left behind by the highwaymen. More than this, it showed clearly that the gang had a highly efficient spy system. The shipment was one of the largest made since the mule-train holdup, and had, supposedly, been surrounded by absolute secrecy.

At this time Wells Fargo had not gained full control of the express business in California. The lost treasure was not Wells Fargo's, but a picked crew of its best detectives was put on the case, with orders to stay on it until the gang was run down and broken up.

There was no trail to be followed, no information could be shaken loose by offers of rewards, and the case seemed hopeless, but Wells Fargo would not quit. It set every agent and clerk in its employ to watching the mails for any suspicious-looking letter, or for any unusual deposit of gold dust. Its drivers, express

messengers, and guards were instructed to watch carefully for another strike by the gang, and to get a good description of some one of its members.

Hundreds of false leads were run down, weeks passed, then a clue was picked up from an intercepted letter, and traced to a hideout near Folsom. A posse was quickly gathered, the hideout surrounded, and a pitched battle was fought. George Skinner, one of the gang, was killed by a Wells Fargo detective. Rattlesnake Dick and three members of his gang were captured and jailed at Auburn. For a few days Wells Fargo and the West breathed easily. Then Rattlesnake

Dick escaped from the jail, reached San Francisco safely, and again disappeared into its underworld.

This time Dick's stay in San Francisco was not long. A few months after his arrival the Vigilance Committee was formed, and the climate of San Francisco became unhealthy for men who had become famous as thieves and robbers. Rattlesnake Dick was flushed out, together with a horde of lesser criminals.

There is little doubt that Richard Barter would have become one of the greatest leaders in the development of the West if he had not, unfortunately, been convicted of a crime he had not committed. For, as Rattlesnake Dick, he built and controlled the first widespread organization for wholesale robbery. Our modern underworld gangs still operate on the pattern he invented and established.

Although the leader and brains of the band, Dick was never a rowdy. And it is doubtful that he himself actually took part in any of the scores of holdups his organization pulled off during the three years he remained Wells Fargo's number one enemy. Dick was not only handsome, brilliant, and exceedingly quick in action, but possessed of remarkable personal magnetism, and he always dressed and spoke like a gentleman. In spite of his reputation as a bad man, he had hundreds of friends throughout the entire Mother Lode country, and he inspired loyalty in every one of them. Most of them would risk their reputations, even their lives, to please him. Although there was seldom a time during the three years of his heyday when Wells Fargo was not offering a reward for information leading to his arrest, there is no record of his ever having been betrayed.

It is claimed that there were more than fifty members of Rattlesnake Dick's gang, but they were not all highwaymen. Scattered from Shasta in the north to Mariposa in the south, there were innkeepers, bartenders, waitresses, and dance-hall girls who were his spies. They kept a sharp ear for any carelessly dropped word of a big gold shipment, the word was quickly passed along the line to Dick's hideout, and the luckless Wells Fargo messenger who was entrusted with the shipment often found himself looking down the barrels of a half-dozen shotguns.

With an organization of this size, and so widely scattered, it was impossible that all the members could know each other, so Dick set up a system of signals and passwords. A stranger might come into a bar, order a drink, and turn the glass halfway around before lifting it to his lips. If the bartender were not a member of the gang it meant nothing to him. If he were, he turned the bottle halfway around before setting it back on the shelf. A waitress might set a stranger's cup down with the handle turned away from him, and he might reach across to turn it back with his left hand. A dance-hall girl or innkeeper might mention that the days were growing longer, or shorter. If the stranger said he hadn't noticed it, the word had been passed. Each knew the other could be trusted and used for passing along information.

For three years the war of wits between Rattlesnake Dick and Wells Fargo, the victim of most of his robberies, raged throughout central California. Each new trick that Dick invented sharpened the wits of the Wells Fargo detectives, and they stuck to his trail like bloodhounds, driving him from hideout to hideout. There was no jail in the mountains strong enough to hold him. It has been claimed that he escaped from every jail in the Mother Lode country. At Auburn he stole the jailer's keys and escaped, though bound in irons from arms to ankles. And after each new jail-break he engineered another spectacular holdup, as if daring Wells Fargo to catch him again.

He would send a gang of his men to stage a mock gun-battle in a town where a big gold deposit had just been made in a Wells Fargo bank. While the sheriff and his deputies ran to stop the battle — and most of the townspeople ran to hide under their beds — others of Dick's gang would pounce upon the bank. Guards would be disarmed before they could raise their shotguns to their shoulders, and the agent would be bullied into opening the vault. The large deposit would be far out in the hills before the sheriff woke up to the fact that he had been buncoed.

As in all wars, neither side won all the battles. Sometimes Dick and his gang made a rich haul and got away with it completely. At other times they were caught and the treasure recovered within a matter of hours. But robbery and breaking jail had become a game with Rattlesnake Dick; wealth was of little importance to him. It is known that the gold from some of his biggest holdups was buried immediately. The lonely hills of the Mother Lode country were his bank, and none but he knew the exact location of his deposits. Many old-timers believe the deposits are still there, locked forever in the strongest deposit vaults ever built — the granite walls of the Sierra Nevada.

No one knows how many holdups were made by Rattlesnake Dick and his gang, but stories of many of them may still be found in copies of old California newspapers.

One morning early in May, 1858, two stagecoaches pulled out of Nevada City for Sacramento, sixty-five miles away. A shotgun guard was sent with each coach, since they were both carrying large shipments of gold dust. And the drivers were given strict orders to stay close to each other, so that one guard might help the other in case of an attempted holdup. I. N. Dawnley, the agent for a Sacramento bank, rode in the front coach. He was carrying twenty thousand dollars' worth of gold dust in a carpetbag. As he climbed into the coach he pushed the carpetbag back under the seat, so that it would not be in the way of the other passengers. Under the guard's feet in the boot of the second coach was a Wells Fargo treasure box. Among other valuables, it held twenty-one thousand dollars' worth of gold.

The stronger and better team of horses was on the front coach, and its load was lighter. For the first five or six miles out of Nevada City the two coaches rolled along at a smart trot, one close behind the other. But when they reached the first long, steep grade the heavily loaded coach in the rear fell a bit farther behind. The gap widened to nearly a quarter-mile by the time the first coach reached the top of the hill, and the second coach was out of sight on the snaking mountain road.

The driver in the lead was looking back over his shoulder when a half-dozen of Rattlesnake Dick's boys leaped out of the brush. As always, the attack was made with such perfect timing that the guard and passengers had no chance to draw their weapons before they were covered by shotguns. And, as always, in a Rattlesnake Dick holdup, they were ordered to throw down their guns, get out, and line up along the roadside while the coach was being ransacked.

Dawnley was not only a brave man, but a clever one. As he stepped out of the coach he said to the highwaymen, "Gentlemen, there is no treasure box on this coach, but there is a coach right behind us with twenty-one thousand dollars' worth of gold in the Wells Fargo treasure box."

One of the bandits jumped up on the wheel and looked into the boot of the coach, where the treasure box was always carried. "He's not lyin', boys! There ain't no box up here," he called down to the rest of the gang.

The sound of the second coach could already be heard as its six-horse team pulled slowly up the mountain road. Anxious to get the first coach out of the way before the second should come in sight, the highwaymen ordered the passengers back inside, and the driver to whip on down the hill quickly.

The robbers were back in hiding before the second coach rounded the last bend in the road, and again they made a perfectly timed holdup. They had lined up the guard, driver, and passengers, thrown down the treasure box, and were rifling the baggage when they heard the pound of horses' hoofs coming fast up the road behind. This could mean only one thing: Wells Fargo had outfoxed them and sent along a mounted guard of riflemen. Quickly smashing the treasure box, they grabbed up the gold pouches and raced away into the brush.

A minute or two after the robbery three riders came pounding around the bend of the road. Two of them were gold buyers who had missed the coaches at their last stop. They had hired horses on which to catch up, and had brought along a man from the livery stable to lead the horses back. Between them they were carrying $16,000 in gold dust.

Wells Fargo detectives finally caught up with Rattlesnake Dick's boys who had stolen the $21,000, but the robbers had let $36,000 get away from them out there on the hilltop. Even at that, they had done better than in some of their holdups, for only a part of the gold was ever recovered.

In August of that same year a stagecoach left Angels Camp for a fast run to Stockton. There was $37,500 in the Wells Fargo treasure box, and a shotgun guard beside the driver. This shipment had been kept a carefully guarded secret, and to avoid any chance of spying, the coach had rolled quietly out of Angels Camp before daylight. It was only two miles out of town when Dick's boys hit it, and they hit it hard. Within two minutes from the time they leaped into the road and shouted, "Holdup!" they had made off into the brush with the $37,500. But they had made the mistake of leaving a telltale trail behind them, and they had made their stickup too close to the town. Within an hour Wells Fargo sleuths were on the job. Before another sunrise the $37,500 was back in the Wells Fargo vaults, and Rattlesnake Dick's boys were in the jailhouse.

From the time Henry Wells had first set the policy, the firm had spared no expense in its effort to run down thieves and see that they were punished. For three years Rattlesnake Dick had led them a merry chase. Although he and his gang had got away with more than a hundred thousand dollars that had never been recovered, Wells Fargo was tightening the loop around them. Its detectives knew where nearly all their hideouts were located, were keeping watch on most of Dick's spies, and had a large number of his followers locked up safely in penitentiaries from which they could not escape. Beyond this, the firm had won the confidence and co-operation of every honest sheriff and deputy in the state. Each day that passed made it harder for Dick and the remnant of his gang to operate.

But Rattlesnake Dick was proud, and he still had confidence in his own ability to outwit or outshoot any sheriff or Wells Fargo man in California. At about eight o'clock on the evening of July 11, 1859, he rode through the main street of Auburn with a member of his gang. Posters offering rewards for both of them — either dead or alive — were tacked to buildings on both sides of the street. But the two riders made no attempt to disguise themselves, and they didn't hurry. Dick was carefully dressed, as always, with well-pressed black trousers, a cream-colored vest, a light gray merino coat, and kid gloves. His whole manner was a dare to anyone who wanted trouble; few sheriffs were fast enough on the draw to

want any part in tangling with him in a man-to-man battle.

George Martin was the exception. He rounded up two deputy sheriffs, Johnson and Crutcher. They saddled their horses quickly, checked the action of their six-shooters, and galloped out of town on the road taken by Dick and his follower. About two miles out they saw the two riders jogging along in the moonlight as if they were just out for a pleasure ride on a warm evening. Johnson, who was riding in front of Martin and Crutcher, shouted, "Halt! Hands up!"

As Rattlesnake Dick turned in his saddle he called back, "What's wanted?" But he didn't wait for an answer. The words were barely out of his mouth before there was a flash from his pistol. For a man turned half around on a trotting horse in semidarkness, his shot was one of the most amazing in history. The bullet cut Johnson's bridle reins in two and shattered his left hand. At almost the same moment there was a second shot, and Martin pitched out of his saddle, stone-dead.

Johnson and Crutcher fought back, shooting as best they could in the moonlight. But, without reins, Johnson couldn't control his frightened horse, and when Crutcher's gun was empty they had to quit the fight.

Auburn was in deep mourning that night. Martin had been one of the best-liked men in town, and it seemed that he had lost his life uselessly. When Johnson and Crutcher quit the fight, Rattlesnake Dick and his man had ridden on as though nothing had happened.

This was the last exhibition of Dick's pride and courage. Early the next morning his body was found at the roadside, more than a mile from the scene of the fight. Two bullets had passed completely through his body, and both of them had struck vital organs. It is almost unbelievable that any man could have ridden so far after receiving two bullet wounds, either of which was bound to be fatal. But Rattlesnake Dick had been an unbelievable man from the time he was seventeen.

5

RATTLESNAKE DICK'S reign as King of the California Highwaymen was longer than that of any other man, but for a while he was outdone by another "gentleman highwayman" who brought terror to the whole mid-section of the state.

Dr. Thomas J. Hodges was born in Rome, Tennessee, and was the son of a fine Southern family. He was a brilliant student in medical school, graduated with honors, and joined the United States Army during the Mexican War. He served well as a non-commissioned officer and was given an honorable discharge at the end of the war.

Word of the gold discovery in California reached Dr. Hodges soon after he was discharged from the Army, and many months before the gold rush was well under way. Not yet having established himself as a civilian doctor, and being a lover of adventure, he headed west.

Dr. Hodges was about twenty-three years old when, in late 1848, he arrived at San Francisco and went straight to the diggings. He was a giant of a man, well over six feet tall, with bull-like shoulders, blue eyes, and a mop of red hair. There was no doubting his strength or courage. Within a few days he had proved that he loved a fight and could lick any man in camp, but he knew nothing of mining and had little taste for hard labor. He prospected lazily and unsuccessfully for a while, then spent most of his time fighting, drinking, and gambling with the roughest and toughest men in the camps.

After seven years in the mining camps Dr. Hodges had nothing to show for his efforts except a nose that was mashed flat to his face — and a fine taste for

whiskey. He abandoned mining entirely when the mountain streams dried up in 1855, and turned his attention to thievery. He was no more successful at this new trade than at prospecting, was convicted of grand theft and sent to prison on Angel Island in San Francisco Bay.

As might have been expected, Dr. Hodges made his friends at Angel Island among the toughest of the prisoners. It was not long until he had escaped, together with five of his newly found friends. Four of them joined him in forming the most vicious gang of thieves and cutthroats ever known in the West. The name "Dr. Hodges" didn't seem quite appropriate for the leader of such a gang, so Hodges dropped it and adopted the name of Tom Bell. Then he led his recruits back to the Mother Lode country — where he was already well acquainted with the toughest element, the most dishonest innkeepers, and the little-known trails through the mountains.

Within a few months after his escape Bell had built his gang to amazing size. His spies were scattered from one end of the Mother Lode to the other, and his gang was already larger than Rattlesnake Dick's.

Although both leaders were thieves and criminals, there was a difference between them. Dick seldom took part in a holdup personally, and his men were under strict orders: their job was to get the Wells Fargo treasure box, but there was to be no wanton killing done in an attempt to get it. They were to respect completely the unwritten law of California highwaymen: stagedrivers and messengers were never to be robbed of their own money or valuables. Dick was gentlemanly in his general behavior, his word was good, he was loyal to his friends, and his friends were loyal to him. Tom Bell was a swaggering, bragging, often drunken, and always a loud-mouthed bully. His only friends were among the most disreputable in the mountains — both men and women — and their loyalty was of the only sort such people know: the sort that can be bought for money.

Tom Bell loved violence. Whenever there was a big holdup to be made he was always in the forefront of his gang. And although he at first claimed to be against wanton killing, he soon got over his scruples. Time and again the first warning of a holdup by one of Bell's gangs was a blast of buckshot from the brush along a lonely roadside.

Within less than a year from the time he escaped from Angel Island, Bell's power had grown so great that he had little fear of any sheriff's posse that could be raised in the mountains. Places that had been his hideouts while he was forming his gang had become his hangouts by the summer of 1856. At these, he and those of his thugs who were not out robbing and stealing spent their time at drinking, gambling, and uproarious roistering.

The location of these hangouts was well known to Wells Fargo's detectives. Time and again they had trapped Bell and his chief lieutenants in them, but were powerless to spring the traps, for Wells Fargo had no authority as a law enforcement agency. Without the co-operation of local sheriffs they could make no attack. But, regardless of Wells Fargo rewards, the sheriffs could not raise posses to attack Bell's hangouts, known to be bristling with half-drunk, trigger-happy gunmen itching for a chance to prove their gang stronger than any law enforcement body in the state.

Tom Bell's favorite hangout was the Western Exchange tavern — called the Hog Ranch by most of the people in Nevada County. This tavern was on the road between Nevada City and Grass Valley. It was, no doubt, owned by Bell, but it was run by Mrs. Hood, alias Mrs. Cullers. She was a fat, redheaded woman who had three redheaded daughters. Tom Bell is said to have been in love with the youngest of them.

Although the Hog Ranch was Bell's favorite hangout, Madam Cole's California House — on the same road, but only twenty-five miles out of Marysville — was the most important. It had many advantages. Stagecoaches from the richest camps and towns in the Mother Lode passed it every day, and more than a few of them carried Wells Fargo treasure boxes.

It was a simple matter for Tom Bell's spies to send word ahead that a rich shipment of gold dust was on its way down from the mountains. The California House was the only inn between Marysville and Rough and Ready, so miners often stopped there for the night. This made it easy for Bell's spies to come and go without arousing too much suspicion of the stagedrivers. Then too, the inn was so located that it would be difficult for a sheriff's posse to attack it by surprise.

Early on the morning of August 12, 1856, the regular stagecoach for Marysville pulled out of Nevada City. To anyone watching it pull away from the Wells Fargo office, the only thing that would have seemed unusual was that four of its ten passengers were Chinamen and one a Negro woman — the wife of a Marysville barber. Of the other five passengers, two wore tall silk hats and were doubtlessly gold buyers or businessmen bound for San Francisco. The other three were dressed in the heavy hobnailed boots, baggy pants, and gray wool shirts of miners.

High on the driver's seat, John Gear gathered the six reins into one ham-like hand, cracked his long whip just above the backs of his lead team, and shouted, "Hud-up! Ha! Ha! Ha!" Beside him Bill Dobson, the shotgun guard, sat tense and alert as the coach rocked and lurched behind the galloping teams. Bill Dobson had good reason to be alert; in the treasure box under his feet there was gold dust worth $100,000.

For August, the morning was cool, and the road to Marysville was downhill most of the way, winding around the shoulders of foothills through dense forests of Sierra pine and fir. John Gear was proud of his six high-spirited bays, and even more proud of his reputation as one of the best stagedrivers in the Sierras. On a cool morning like this there was little need to spare the horses, and he planned to make a record run to Marysville. Shouting and cracking his whip, he took the big Concord coach thundering down the narrow, twisting road with skill that was almost unbelievable. At the hairpin curves his foot hit the long brake lever at the last possible moment, skidding the wheels to within inches of the drop-off, but losing no more momentum than was absolutely necessary. At a speed such as this it would take a small army of highwaymen to pull a holdup.

It was not yet noon when John Gear swung the reeling coach around a bend and came within sight of the California House. At just that moment one of his passengers, dressed as a miner, stuck his head from the coach window and shouted that he wanted to get off at the inn. John kicked the brake lever down hard and brought the plunging six-horse team to a stop in front of the well-known hangout. The second his passenger's feet hit the ground he cracked his whip and galloped the team away; the California House was no place at which to stop very long when there was $100,000 in the treasure box.

The "miner" galloped for the front door of the inn about as fast as John's bays galloped down the road toward Marysville. The coach was barely out of sight when Tom Bell and six of his toughest followers ran from the back door of the inn. Three of them were thugs who had escaped with him from Angel Island, two were San Francisco murderers driven out by the Vigilantes, and the sixth was a Mexican by the name of Juan Fernandez. They dashed for the corral, threw saddles on their horses, and raced away on a game trail through the timber. The road below the California House swept around a hillside in a wide curve to the crossing at Dry Creek, deep in the bottom of a rocky gulch. The game trail crossed the top of the hill, then plunged down the boulder-strewn gulch, cutting the distance to the crossing in half.

To avoid upsetting the heavy stagecoach in making the rough crossing, John Gear was obliged to pull his horses to a walk. He had put the lead team across the bottom of the creek bed, and it was scrambling up the far bank when Tom Bell and his thugs spurred their horses into the roadway. Their guns were pointed at Gear, Dobson, and the passengers, and Bell shouted for Dobson to throw down the box. Dobson's answer was the most daring ever made by an express guard in California. With five guns pointed at him, the frightened horses plunging, and the stagecoach rocking wildly, he snapped his shotgun to his shoulder and fired at Bell. That load of buckshot would have cut a man in half at such short range, but Dobson had no time to take aim. The blast knocked Bell from his horse, but he was not badly wounded.

Before Bell hit the ground Dobson had dropped his empty shotgun and yanked the Colts from his holsters. The bandits' horses were as frightened as those of the stage teams. They reared and whirled as their riders shot wildly at the coach. Dobson had no time to take aim, but shot at the lurching targets as fast as he could thumb the triggers of his guns.

At the sound of the first shot the Chinamen had leaped from the stage and scuttled away into the brush, but the two miners and the silk-hatted gentlemen opened fire immediately. The barber's wife sat bolt upright and stock-still, too frightened to move.

Men who gather in gangs and follow a vicious leader are usually cowards, and the tougher they act the more cowardly they often are. Bell's henchmen were about as tough a lot as ever gathered together. With him to lead them they could put up a great show of bravery, but without him they were no better than a pack of coyotes. And Tom Bell had been knocked out of the fight at Dobson's first shot. As he pulled

himself to his knees and dived back into the brush, five of his brave henchmen were quick to follow him; they'd had all the gun fight they had any taste for.

Fernandez was the only bandit left in the battle. He spurred his horse alongside the coach, firing as the animal reared and pitched. Dobson returned his fire, shot him from the saddle and shouted to John Gear to drive on. The coach didn't move. In his excitement, Dobson shouted at Gear that if he didn't drive on he'd shoot him. It was only then he noticed

that Gear had been shot through the forearm and couldn't handle the six frightened horses. Grabbing the whip and reins, Dobson poured leather onto the horses' backs and sent them plunging and galloping up out of the creek bottom. At the first lurch of the coach, the barber's wife pitched forward from her straight sitting position — stone-dead, with a bullet through her brain.

It is very probable that a man might have been killed in that attempted holdup without causing any great excitement. But in 1856 honest women were considered sacred in California, and the barber's wife had been an honest woman. Her wanton killing aroused the anger of every honorable Californian, and sheriffs were quickly able to raise posses of picked marksmen to tackle Bell's gang.

With law enforcement now assured, Wells Fargo put its whole detective force into the mountains. Before nightfall Tom Bell's hangouts were surrounded and stormed, many of his followers were captured and a few killed, but Bell managed to shoot his way out and escape. The sheriffs and their posses ranged through the foothills like packs of bloodhounds in search of him, but Tom Bell seemed to have disappeared as if by magic.

The French have a saying, *Cherchez la femme* ("Find the woman"), and the Wells Fargo detectives took this for their battle cry. Fat Mrs. Hood and her three redheaded daughters had disappeared from the Hog Ranch. Wherever they were to be found, Tom Bell would probably be found somewhere nearby.

California is a big state and there are thousands of places in it where four redheaded women might hide. But the Wells Fargo men went methodically at searching out every possible hiding place. Rewards for information were offered; storekeepers, innkeepers, bartenders, and miners were questioned. Dozens of leads were run down, but each led to the wrong redheaded woman. August passed, and September. Then a clue was found that led them far up the Merced River. Near the spot where the Merced now rushes out of the Yosemite National Park in tumbling cascades, the women were found holed up in a little cabin, far back from the trail. Their loyalty was equal to that of Tom's other friends. To save themselves from possible arrest they disclosed Tom's hideout: he was to be found in the next canyon toward the east.

On October 6, the sheriff of Calaveras, together with nine picked deputies, rode into the canyon. They expected to find Bell's hideout bristling with gunmen, and they rode at the alert, ready for a gun battle at any moment. The sheriff was in the lead. As he rounded a twist in the trail he came suddenly upon Tom Bell. He was seated comfortably on his horse, one leg hooked around the saddle horn, and talking with a Mexican. He was so sure of being safely hidden that he had become careless. And he was so completely surprised that before he could make a move to defend himself ten guns were pointing at his head — with the hammer thumbed back on every one of them. None of the posse had ever seen Bell, but there was no mistaking him. No other man in California had his nose smashed so flat against his face.

If Tom Bell had drawn a weapon, or even made a move to draw one, the sheriff and his deputies would have been justified in killing him on the spot. But, since he was taken prisoner without a fight, he was entitled to a fair trial in the courts, regardless of the fact that he was known to be a wanton murderer. This the sheriff of Calaveras knew well, but he also knew that there were still judges in California from whom a not-guilty verdict could be bought or frightened. Beyond this, he knew that Bell had already escaped from the strongest prison in the state and that, if given a chance, he'd doubtlessly do it again. Rather than risk Bell's going unpunished for his past crimes, or escaping to commit others, the sheriff exceeded his authority and took the law into his own hands. Tom was given four hours in which to prepare for the hereafter. Then, just as dusk was falling, he was strung up on the stoutest limb of a nearby tree.

6

WHILE the Wells Fargo detectives and messengers were carrying on their relentless war against Tom Bell and Rattlesnake Dick, the company was continuing to tighten its hold on the stagecoach and express business in the West. The big stampede of the gold rush had passed, few new strikes were being made, but hard-rock and hydraulic mining had replaced the gold-pan prospectors, and the Mother Lode still turned out a steady flow of the yellow metal.

In the early years of the stampede scores of independent stage lines had sprung up, but the panic of 1855 and losses to the bandit gangs and highwaymen had been too much for them. One by one, the owners had sold out to Wells Fargo. By 1859 its only important rival was the California Stage Company. The stirring races between the competing lines had stopped with the panic, but they were soon to start all over again.

The lure of gold is a disease from which some men never recover. As the gold dust in the California stream beds was exhausted, those who had the fever prospected higher into the Sierra Nevada, across the summit, and down the eastern rampart. There, in the barren foothills of western Utah — now Nevada — they discovered the richest deposit of gold and silver that the world has ever known. It was called the Comstock Lode. From its Ophir mine alone $145,000,000 in gold and silver was taken in less than twelve years. Within weeks the barren hills were overrun with prospectors. Camps and towns sprang up like mushrooms.

Within a year Virginia City, Nevada, had a population of 20,000, and had taken away San Francisco's reputation as the wickedest city in the world. More than half the buildings on the one main street were saloons. The dance halls and gambling houses ran full blast twenty-four hours a day, and murders were so common they caused little excitement. The thunderous stamping mills processing the ore belched clouds of black smoke from their chimneys, and countless bars of gold and silver poured from their smelting pots.

To get this precious metal to the government mint in San Francisco, it had to be carried across the mile-and-a-half-high Sierra Nevada Mountains in stagecoaches. Thousands of gold-crazed prospectors clamored for the fastest possible transportation to the new bonanza. Thousands of tons of food, clothing mine supplies, and building materials had to be hauled across the mountains from the coast, and millions of dollars' worth of treasure brought back. The cream of the business would go to the firm that could furnish the fastest and safest service — speed for the passengers and freight, safety for the treasure. Wells Fargo was forced to race its competitor, the California Stage Company, for the business.

Wells Fargo's first office in Virginia City was a tent on C Street. But on the other side of the street its two-story banking and express building was going up as fast as bricks could be laid. It was the finest building in the city, and was no sooner finished than stage-coaches lined up in front of it three abreast, loading passengers and treasure for San Francisco. Down the street more coaches were being loaded at the station of the California Stage Company. Within minutes whips would crack, six-horse teams would race down C Street as the pedestrians scattered, and the race up and over the mountains would be on.

Before the races between the two great rivals were begun, the trip from Sacramento to Virginia City required three days and two nights. When the races were at their height, the time was cut to less than thirteen hours. In one of the most spectacular of these the California Company's driver covered the distance in twelve hours and eighteen minutes. Wells Fargo's driver raced in three minutes behind him.

Within less than two years after the Comstock Lode was discovered the War Between the States broke out. The costs of war were tremendous, and the Union needed the gold and silver from this great natural treasury as rapidly as it could be dug from the earth. The number of stamping mills and smelters was doubled. Hordes of miners ripped deep into Mount Davidson night and day. Wells Fargo pressed into service every stagecoach that could be bought, and the traffic on the road between Virginia City and Sacramento was equal to that between Washington and Baltimore.

On the night of June 3, 1864, fifteen heavily loaded coaches from Virginia City careened down the twisting mountain road on their way to Sacramento. In the lead and setting a fast pace drove Ned Blair. At his feet were the Wells Fargo treasure box and four heavy bags of silver — each of them worth more than $2000. In his coach two women and seven men jostled one another as the swaying vehicle skidded around sharp curves. Five more men, clinging for their lives, rode on top. Close behind drove Charley Watson, carrying fourteen passengers and four bags of silver bullion.

Ned Blair had made one of his fastest drives down the treacherous American River canyon. As his coach rolled out from between the high canyon walls and into the foothills he glanced over his shoulder at the moon, then eased up a bit on the galloping horses. It couldn't be later than ten o'clock, so there was no need to crowd them on the uphill pull to Thirteen-Mile House. From there the road was good, and downhill all the way to Placerville; he could easily make it before midnight, his scheduled time.

Ned had swung his lead team wide for the last sharp curve before reaching Thirteen-Mile House when a shout came from the bushes along the roadside: "Pull up, or we'll fire!"

There was no need for Blair to pull up. A half-dozen masked men leaped from the brush and grabbed the horses' bridles. Another six or eight loomed in the moonlight, their guns covering Ned and his passengers. From among the highwaymen a voice called in a gentlemanly tone, "We'll detain you but a moment. All we want is Wells Fargo's treasure."

While the robbers were ransacking Ned's coach, Charley Watson drove up from behind. He had barely pulled his rearing horses to a stop when the leader of the holdup band came toward his coach, bowed, and said, "Gentlemen and ladies — for I see some of the fairer sex among you — I will tell you who we are. We are not ordinary robbers, but a company of Confederate soldiers. We do not prey on private citizens. All we want is Wells Fargo's bullion, to help us recruit for our army."

Charley Watson was not used to such courtesy from highwaymen, and he was not in sympathy with the Confederacy. He threw down the two bags of silver nearest him, and called, "That's all, mister!" But the "Confederate soldiers" were not willing to take a Yankee's word for it. One of them climbed up to investigate, threw down the remaining bags, and called to his companions to search the coach thoroughly. While this was going on, their leader was very gallant in his behavior to all the ladies, and apologized for any inconvenience he and his men might have caused them. When the search of the coach had been completed he politely handed Charley Watson a receipt for the treasure that had been confiscated:

This is to certify that I have received from Wells Fargo & Co. the sum of $——— cash, for the purpose of outfitting recruits enlisted in California for the Confederate States Army.

R. HENRY INGRAM
Captain Commanding Co., C.S.A.
June, 1864

Then, with a bow to the ladies, he told the drivers of both coaches that they might drive on.

Ned Blair and Charley Watson needed no urging. They put whips to their teams and raced for Thirteen-Mile House, where there was a telegraph line to Placerville. As Ned pulled his horses to a sliding stop in front of the inn, he jumped from his seat and ran in to telegraph news of the holdup to the Wells Fargo agent at Placerville. His passengers followed him as fast as they could scramble out of the coach, but only as far as the barroom. It seemed that the gentlemen all felt a need to quiet their jangled nerves. Before they could be served, Charley Watson and his passengers joined the crowd. The passengers pressed against the bar two-deep, shouting to the bartender for service, and arguing with each other as to whether there had been fourteen or fourteen hundred Confederate soldiers.

When the hubbub was at its height two men in miners' clothing strolled in. They didn't mix with the crowd at the bar, but circled around it, went to the desk, and told the clerk they wanted rooms for the night. Charley Watson, too, had not mixed with the crowd, but waited near the desk for his passengers to finish quieting their nerves. As the men at the desk asked for rooms he thought he recognized a familiar tone in one of their voices. He listened more closely. If he wasn't badly mistaken he had heard those same tones when the highwayman who climbed onto his coach had called to his companions. Waiting until the men had gone to their rooms, Charley hurried to the telegraph operator and wired his suspicions to the Placerville agent.

By the time Ned Blair and Charley Watson had rounded up their excited passengers and driven to Placerville, Wells Fargo had posted a reward of $1000 for the recovery of the treasure, and $300 for each of the highwaymen. This made a total of more than $5000 and was enough to spur any sheriff in the mountains into action. Sheriff Rogers had already gathered a posse and was racing out of town toward Thirteen-Mile House. The two "Confederate soldiers" whom Charley Watson had suspected were surprised and arrested before they could leap out of bed and grab their guns.

At daylight a study of tracks at the scene of the holdup showed that the band had scattered. Deputy Staples and Constable Ranney discovered the trail of six horses that had been spurred at a fast pace up the winding canyon of the Consumnes River. Twelve miles up the canyon was the Somerset House, an inn kept for miners by Mrs. Reynolds. The highwaymen would, no doubt, have stopped for a few hours' sleep, or at least for breakfast. Staples and Ranney took a short cut through the hills and approached the inn cautiously. Mrs. Reynolds was in the kitchen cooking breakfast. Constable Ranney hissed to attract her attention, motioned her to him, and asked if any strangers had passed that way since midnight. She nodded toward her front bedroom and whispered, "Six of 'em."

Deputy Staples showed more courage than judgment. With his shotgun cocked and Constable Ranney close behind him, he kicked open the door of the room and shouted, "You are my prisoners!"

The door was barely halfway open when a shotgun bellowed from inside the darkened room. The blast of buckshot riddled Deputy Staples, killing him almost instantly. But in that instant he pulled the trigger, spraying the room with shot and wounding one of the bandits. The same shot that killed Deputy Staples knocked Constable Ranney out of the fight but did not kill him. Leaving their wounded partner to crawl away as best he could, the highwaymen ran for their horses, mounted, and raced away toward the high Sierras.

Deputy Staples had been one of the most popular men in Placerville. When word of his death reached the town a posse of fifty men was formed, and by nightfall they had brought in the man he had wounded, together with a bar of silver from the Thirteen-Mile holdup. The man identified himself as Tom Poole, a former undersheriff of Monterey County. He swore that he knew nothing about the robbery and had only fallen in with the highwaymen that morning when they stopped at Mrs. Reynolds' inn. Charley Watson listened to his voice and recognized it immediately. The Southern drawl was gone, but the voice was that of the bandit leader who had signed the receipt as Captain Ingram.

Certain now that the holdup at Thirteen-Mile House had nothing to do with the Confederacy, the posse spurred back into the mountains. It picked up the trail of the five highwaymen who had escaped, and followed it as fast as their horses could travel in the rough mountains. But it soon became evident that the robbers were excellently mounted and knew they were being followed. Winding, twisting, and changing direction from day to day, they made their way southward and toward the summit of the Sierras. Sheriff Rogers and his deputies stuck to the trail, but each day they fell farther behind and the trail grew fainter. Far south, in Calaveras County, the trail was lost completely, and Sheriff Rogers was forced to give up the chase.

James B. Hume, who became Wells Fargo's most famous chief detective, knew nothing of the holdup at Thirteen-Mile House. He was out in the rugged mountains of Calaveras County, doggedly following the trail of a gang that had held up another stage. Jim Hume and his men were close upon the heels of their gang at about the time Sheriff Rogers lost the trail of the "Confederate soldiers." All afternoon Hume had been gaining on the outlaws he was trailing, and had driven them into a box canyon. Soon after moonrise he forced them to abandon their horses and loot and take to the rugged mountainside afoot. Shortly before midnight he had driven them nearly to the summit of the mountain and was spreading out his men to surround them.

By the merest of chance, the fleeing "Confederate soldiers" were camped at the summit of this same mountain. From their high lookout they had watched Sheriff Rogers turn back. Then, weary and sure they had made their escape, they settled down for a good night's rest. Horses were unsaddled, hobbled, and turned loose to graze. Supper was cooked, blankets spread, and four of the outlaws went peacefully to sleep, leaving the fifth to act as lookout. He, too, was weary from the long chase. As the moon rose higher

he drowsed. Suddenly he was awakened by a sound on the mountainside just below. Rubbing the sleep from his eyes he peered into the jumble of moonlit boulders. There, ducking cautiously from shadow to shadow and holding their guns at the ready, he saw men coming toward him.

These were the bandits who were trying to escape Jim Hume, but the "Confederate" lookout was sure they must be Sheriff Rogers's posse. With a wild shout he woke his partners, and together they raced down the far side of the mountain, leaving their horses, blankets, food, ammunition, and a bar of silver taken in the Thirteen-Mile holdup.

Upon hearing the shouts from the mountaintop the robbers of the Georgetown stage believed that Hume and his posse had them completely surrounded and were closing in for the kill. In panic they threw down their guns and surrendered. Jim Hume recognized them immediately as cowardly small-time thieves who had recently escaped from the Placerville jail. Since the treasure they had stolen from the Wells Fargo box had already been recovered, he wasted little time on them. They were quickly shackled together and a single deputy was sent to take them back to the jail, while Hume and the rest of his posse went on to investigate the shouting at the mountaintop.

The great detective is the one who considers every scrap of evidence in the solving of a crime, and Jim Hume was one of the greatest. By the time he had completed his examination of the "Confederate soldiers' " camp he needed no one to tell him there had been a big holdup on the Virginia City stage route, that the five men he had surprised were only a part of the robber band, or that there doubtlessly had been a killing. Beyond this, he was reasonably certain as to where the highwaymen had come from, where they were headed for, and how they could be captured.

Hume knew the abandoned bar of silver to be from a Virginia City smelter, and reason told him that it was only a very small part of the treasure stolen, for silver bullion was always shipped in large quantities. Still, he knew that this single bar was all these five bandits had been carrying. Such bars of silver were heavy; tracks showed that the bandits had left their camp at a frantic run, and no man could run in that way if he were carrying a bar of silver. There could be only two possible reasons for the single bar: either the bulk of the treasure had been buried, or these five men were only a small part of a large gang which had split up, and a single bar was their share of the loot. The fact that the bandits had panicked led Hume to believe a murder had been committed; the punishment for stage robbery was not great enough to have caused them such fright.

An examination of the horses and equipment told Jim Hume the rest of the story. The horses were of fine Mexican stock, and there were very few such horses in central California. The saddle blankets, too, were Mexican, but the few articles of clothing were definitely American. All the saddlebags were bulging; packed with enough dried food to last five men a month, and with enough ammunition for a cavalry troop.

The amount of ammunition was further proof that this was part of a large gang, for five men could not have used so much in a ten-day battle. The quantity of food carried showed them to be on a long journey. The horses and blankets had certainly come from somewhere near the Mexican border, but the clothing showed the men to be Americans. Putting these clues together, Jim Hume reasoned that the gang was from the Los Angeles area. This would account for their being so far south of the Virginia City road. If they had not lost their horses and supplies they would, doubtlessly, have remained hidden in the mountains until they were well beyond the settlements in the San Joaquin Valley. Now that they were afoot and without supplies, they must get out of the mountains as quickly as possible. The chances were ten to one that they would try to rejoin the rest of the gang on its way home. The meeting place would certainly be at or near San Jose, for it was there that the Los

Angeles road branched to the north and south of San Francisco Bay.

With his problem worked out, Jim Hume made no attempt to follow the trail of the bandits in darkness. The night could better be spent in resting his men and the horses. Next morning he returned to the box canyon for his own horses, circled the mountain and took the easiest and most direct course toward San Jose, making no effort to pick up the trail of the fleeing highwaymen. To do so would only waste time, for — if he had reasoned correctly — the bandits would also take the easiest and most direct course.

Within an hour Jim Hume's judgment was proved to be right. In a narrow canyon footprints were found in a dry creek bed. They showed the five highwaymen to be traveling together at a steady walk, one of them limping. Hume slowed his posse and moved on cautiously. If these frightened men were pressed too closely they would certainly scatter and, in those wild mountains, be almost impossible to run down. If not pressed they would stay together and head for the closest point on the Los Angeles road, somewhere near San Jose.

Day after day Jim Hume and his posse followed the five "Confederate soldiers" down the gorges of the Sierra Nevada Mountains, across the San Joaquin Valley, over the Diablo Mountains, and on toward the southern end of San Francisco Bay. In hope that they might lead him to a rendezvous with the rest of the gang, he made no attempt to capture them, and followed only closely enough that the trail might not be lost. The trail ended at an old farmhouse on the Los Angeles road, near San Jose. There the band was surrounded. One of them was killed in a pitched battle, and the other four surrendered. In an effort to escape full punishment for their crime, those who surrendered named and described every member of the entire gang, identifying Tom Poole as their leader.

With the descriptions broadcast to every sheriff in central California, the whole gang was quickly rounded up and brought to trial. Tom Poole, who had signed the receipt as Captain Ingram, was hanged for the killing of Deputy Staples. The others were convicted of robbery and sent to the penitentiary for long terms. Before their trial they had taken Wells Fargo agents to a spring near Thirteen-Mile House. There they had dug up all the treasure taken in the holdup — with the exception of the two bars of silver already recovered. Slowly but surely, Wells Fargo was teaching highwaymen that robbing their treasure boxes was not a profitable business.

7

DURING the War Between the States and the few years that followed, Wells Fargo built its stagecoach business into the greatest in the world. Its lines stretched from the Missouri River to the Pacific, and from Canada deep into Mexico. Day and night the canyons of the Sierras echoed the sound of galloping hoofs and skidding wheels, as Wells Fargo coaches rushed millions upon millions of dollars' worth of gold and silver from the Comstock Lode to the San Francisco Mint. But the heyday of stagecoaching was already drawing to its close.

With the completion of the transcontinental railroad there was no longer need for the overland stages between the Missouri and California. And although Wells Fargo treasure boxes still carried millions in gold and silver from the Comstock Lode, they rode in express cars over the railroads. Then too, most of the gold had been washed from the California sand bars during the war, and most of the placer mines worked out. Many of the booming mining camps of the 1850's had become ghost towns — the windows of their ten-antless buildings staring out across the creeks and rivers like the unseeing eyes of the blind. Stagecoaches still rolled between the larger towns, but shotgun guards no longer rode beside the drivers, and there was seldom any great treasure in the Wells Fargo box.

The heyday of the California highwaymen passed with that of the stagecoach and the heavily loaded treasure boxes, but Black Bart, most famous of them all, was yet to rob his first coach.

On a bright July morning of 1875, John Shine whipped his four-horse team out of Sonora on his regular stage run to Copperopolis and Milton. At his feet the Wells Fargo box bounced and rattled, its treasure of $300 too light to hold it steady. One of his five well-dressed passengers was a woman, and two of the men were evidently gold-dust buyers, for they were armed and carried carpetbags.

Shine kept his horses at a fast pace until he reached the Stanislaus River. There he made a short stop at "Grandma" Rolleri's inn for coffee, then crossed the river at Reynolds Ferry. With the ferry crossing safely made, he lolled back and let the horses set their own pace up Funk's Hill. As they neared the crest John sat idly recalling the twenty years he had driven that route, back to the days when Funk's Hill had been known as the robbers' roost of the West. There had been a time when a week seldom passed without some highwayman holding up a coach on that long, slow pull. Those were the days when the gold camps along the Stanislaus were booming and the Wells Fargo boxes loaded with dust to the cover, but they were past and gone. There hadn't been a holdup on Funk's Hill since . . .

Suddenly John Shine's reverie was broken by the rearing and plunging of his frightened horses. Instinctively he jerked to attention and pulled them to a stop. For a moment he thought he was seeing the ghost of one of those old-time highwaymen. A tall, gaunt figure had slipped from behind a boulder at the roadside and crouched in front of the lead team, aiming a double-barreled shotgun steadily at Shine's head. The highwayman was covered by a white linen duster, and from within the flour sack that was pulled down over his head a deep, hollow voice commanded, "Throw down the box!"

In his surprise, John was a bit slow in reaching for the Wells Fargo box, and one of his passengers shouted, "Drive on!"

John Shine didn't drive. The muzzle of that shotgun was being held too steadily, and the deep voice boomed, "Keep your eyes on them, boys, and be ready with both barrels! If they dare to shoot, give them a solid volley!"

Driver Shine glanced quickly along the roadside. He could have sworn he saw six or seven shotguns

poked out through the bushes. He wasted no time in tossing down the box and calling to his passengers, "No use trying to do anything; he's got a gang with him. If you want to live, don't monkey with your guns!"

As the Wells Fargo box hit the roadway the highwayman stood up, looking to be at least six feet tall. Still pointing his gun at Shine he came back toward the coach with a quick, springy step and demanded, "Throw down the mail sacks!"

"They're in the baggage boot at the back," Shine told him.

The lady passenger panicked when she saw the highwayman coming back toward the coach. Fearing for her life, she threw her purse at his feet. He picked it up, bowed, and passed it back through an open coach window. "Madam," he said, "I do not wish your money. In that respect I honor only the good offices of Wells Fargo."

Without hurrying, he took the mail sacks from the boot, and called into the brush, "That will be all, boys!" Then he stepped back to the roadside and said jovially to Shine, "Hurry along now, my friend, and good luck to you."

Weird holdups were no novelty to James B. Hume, chief of Wells Fargo's detective force, but this one had them all beaten. There could be no doubt that this highwayman was well educated, intelligent, and young. The amount lost in the holdup was not large, but if such a man were heading a large robber band, Wells Fargo might be in for some rough going. The gang must be run down quickly, regardless of cost. Wells Fargo posted a big reward for any member of the gang, particularly for its leader, and Hume hurried to the scene of the holdup. By getting there quickly, he believed, he could easily pick up the trail of so large a gang. If not, he could certainly run down the leader. Now that the gold rush was past, few strangers came into the Mother Lode country. A tall, thin young man who spoke excellent English in a deep voice would be spotted quickly.

When Jim Hume reached Funk's Hill he found the "shotguns" still pointed at the road from the manzanita bushes. They were only sticks, poked through the bushes in such a way that, at a quick glance, they looked like shotguns. Whoever this strange highwayman was, he must have a fine sense of humor, and he must be something of a braggart. Those sticks had surely been left as a joke on his victims, and as a boast that he had pulled the holdup alone.

At the side of the road, Hume found the Wells Fargo box with the padlocked cover battered off, and beside it a rusty ax. Nearby there were two mail sacks, empty and slit in the form of a *T*. That was all the evidence to be found. Hume searched every foot of earth along the hillside, but could find no single track, or any place where a getaway horse had been tied. No one in the nearby towns had seen a tall, deep-voiced stranger in months.

Five months passed with nothing heard from the ghostlike highwayman. Then a coach from San Juan to Marysville, a hundred miles north of Funk's Hill, was held up. There was no doubt as to who the holdup man had been. After another five months an identical holdup was made on the Roseburg (Oregon) to Yreka (California) coach, more than two hundred miles farther north. As in both previous holdups Jim Hume could find no tracks, no clues, and no one who had seen a tall, deep-voiced stranger.

It was fourteen months before the phantom highwayman struck again, but that time he was careful to leave a definite clue behind. One afternoon in August, 1877, two coaches rolled over the low hills along the California coast, on their way to Point Arena from Russian River towns. Since this was not mining country, there was no Wells Fargo box on the first coach, and the one on the second held only $300. The driver of the first coach thought he saw a movement in the brush as he reached the crest of a hill. He quickly put the whip to his horses and galloped them down the far side. As the second driver neared the hilltop a tall figure, disguised in duster and flour sack, stepped from behind a boulder and crouched before the horses. By this time the reputation of the phantom highwayman had spread from one end of California to the other, and the driver needed no urging to throw down the Wells Fargo box and mail sacks.

The next passer-by found no sticks poked into the bushes to resemble shotguns, but on the back of a waybill left in the smashed Wells Fargo box there was a note:

> Driver, give my respects to our friend, the other driver; but I really had a notion to hang my old disguise hat on his weather eye.
>
> Respectfully,
> B. B.

For a year Jim Hume and his men kept up their search for a tall, well-educated stranger with a deep voice. Then, in the Feather River canyon of the Sierras, the phantom made two strikes in succession. Again a jeering clue was left on a waybill in the smashed Wells Fargo treasure box. This time the jest was written in verse, each line in a different style of handwriting, and it was signed:

> *Here I lay me down to sleep*
> *To wait the coming morrow,*
> *Perhaps success, perhaps defeat,*
> *And everlasting sorrow.*

Let come what will I'll try it on,
My condition can't be worse;
And if there's money in that box
'Tis munny in my purse.
                BLACK BART, the Po8

Two months later the self-styled poet (or as he called it, "Po-eight") struck twice more in rapid-fire succession, both times at Ukiah, back across the state and near the coast. His strikes were as unpredictable as lightning, as widely scattered, and as closely followed by thunder. But the thundering was done by the press. Following each holdup, newspapers all over the state demanded that the "bloodthirsty criminal" be captured and hanged immediately. Mothers kept children close to their skirts, and travelers on the roads went armed to the teeth, but there seemed to be little cause for alarm. Black Bart had never yet hurt anyone, and his only robberies had been of mailbags and Wells Fargo treasure boxes.

With each new outburst from the newspapers the local sheriffs were driven into a show of action, and Wells Fargo was driven nearly to distraction. But there seemed to be little that any of them could do, for although Black Bart's flour sack and linen duster had become famous, no one had the least idea what the man inside the disguise looked like.

Mendocino County, in which Ukiah is located, is

still sparsely populated. It lies along the coast, midway between San Francisco Bay and the Oregon border, and its low but rugged mountains are covered by dense redwood forests. From Ukiah the Eel River flows northward, and the Russian River southward. At the time Black Bart held up the Ukiah coaches there were a few lumbering towns along the coast and rivers, and a few farmers had settled in the valleys. The mountains to the east of the rivers were uninhabited by whites. The Indians lived there as they had lived for centuries, hunting their game with bows and arrows. Except for the Apaches, these Indians were the finest trackers in the world. They needed no footprints to follow, but read a trail unerringly by every broken twig, turned pebble, or bit of matted grass.

The sheriff of Mendocino County was friendly with the Indians and knew their ability as trackers. When Black Bart made his strikes at Ukiah, Jim Hume had the sheriff bring in several of the best Indian trackers. They quickly picked up the trail that no white man was able to see, followed it for sixty miles northward, then lost it completely. But in that sixty miles they learned more about Black Bart than white men had been able to learn in three years.

They found that he was an excellent woodsman and mountaineer, knew the country thoroughly, and could slip through the forests almost as tracklessly as a fox. Beyond this, he was a tireless walker, did no hunting

or cooking, and lived on crackers and sugar. These he carried rolled in a single blanket, together with a sawed-off shotgun which he dismounted at the breech. He had covered the entire sixty miles over extremely rugged mountains in three days, and had held his course almost due northward. The man was not so tall as he had been reported to be, probably not over five feet and eight or nine inches.

Even though the Indians had lost Black Bart's trail, Jim Hume now had something he believed he could work with. He rushed a force of his best detectives to the place where Bart's trail had been lost. There he

scattered them to hunt out everyone living within fifty miles and to question them regarding any strangers. Weeks passed, and the only report brought in was that of a kindly traveling preacher who had stopped for a meal at Mrs. McCreary's farmhouse near the Eel River. Even so remote a clue could not be passed over, so Jim Hume went to talk with Mrs. McCreary.

When Hume suggested that the man who had stopped at her house might be Black Bart, Mrs. McCreary became indignant and answered his questions grudgingly. No, the man hadn't exactly said he was a preacher, but she'd known it from his "intellectual conversation," and his hands were "slender and genteel like a preacher's." Besides that, he was an elderly gentleman and poor. His coat and derby hat were far from new, and his shoes had been slit across the joint as if to ease his bunions.

Mrs. McCreary's daughter was more co-operative. She said the man was about two inches taller than she, stood straight as a ramrod, and his hair, beard, and mustache were gray. The mustache was large, but the beard was only a tuft on his chin. His eyes were brilliant blue, set deep under heavy brows that gave them a piercing look, but still they were kindly. Everything about the old gentleman had been kindly. He laughed and joked as he ate, and she had noticed that two of his front teeth were missing.

Yes, his voice was deep, but not rough. A blanket roll? Yes, but there couldn't have been a shotgun wrapped inside it. It had been no larger than two blankets rolled together, and not more than two feet long. He carried it slung across his back. No, she hadn't noticed which way he went when he left, probably toward the road that ran north and south through the valley.

It seemed improbable to Jim Hume that the man who had stopped at the McCreary farm could be the phantom highwayman. Still, there were the deep voice and the blanket roll, and the height was about the same that the Indians had reported. The derby hat might account for his looking taller in his disguise. With the flour sack pulled down over it his height would be increased several inches. Then too, the girl had mentioned the man's laughing and joking. It would be this sort of a man who would leave jeering verses and sign them "Black Bart, the Po8." Jim Hume carefully filed every detail of his talk with Mrs. McCreary and her daughter, then waited for Black Bart to strike again.

During the next two years Black Bart made seven holdups in which he robbed the mails and Wells Fargo treasure boxes. Following each of them, Jim Hume moved in with his men to comb the area, but each holdup was as baffling as those before it. No trail could be picked up, and no one found who had seen a suspicious-appearing stranger with a deep voice. This would have been discouraging to most men, but not to Jim Hume. He believed he saw a pattern emerging. Black Bart had made two holdups in 1875, one in '76, one in '77, four in '78, three in '79, and now four in 1880. Between most of these holdups Bart had leapfrogged a hundred miles or more across the northern third of California. But in three cases he had made a pair of holdups in the same area and in quick succession. In none of them had the amount stolen been more than $500. Whenever the holdups had been made in pairs the amount taken in the first one had been very small. It was evident that this highwayman held up stages only when he needed money to live on, and he had taken no more than would support a single man.

It would have been much cheaper for Wells Fargo to let this strange highwayman continue robbing treasure boxes than to spend many thousands of dollars in an attempt to catch him. But Wells Fargo's policy had always been to run down and punish highwaymen who robbed their treasure boxes, regardless of cost. Jim Hume kept doggedly at his task, moving his men to the scene of each holdup and questioning everyone living within fifty miles. Following a holdup near Redding his thoroughness was rewarded.

In the foothills of the Trinity Mountains he found a rancher who said a stranger had come to his cabin a few days before and asked for breakfast. This had been an elderly gentleman whose hair was almost entirely gray. He had a big white mustache, a little tuft of gray chin whiskers, bright blue eyes under heavy brows, and two front teeth missing. He was afoot and carried nothing but a small blanket roll.

By this time Black Bart had become a legendary figure in California, and many people believed him to be supernatural. Jim Hume had no such idea; just the opposite. He was now positive he had a good description of the phantom highwayman, and that the old rascal's absolute naturalness was the cause of his being so hard to run down. He had only two unnatural qualities. One was his ability to get away from the scene of a holdup without leaving tracks. The other was the fact that a man of this type should have the courage to be a highwayman.

The robber's description, together with his leap-frogging and the fact that a second holdup in the same area always followed an unprofitable one, led Hume to make a second deduction: the highwayman lived in a large city, probably San Francisco. When in need of money he simply made a trip to some distant town, held up a stage — or two if necessary — then returned to live as a well-respected citizen until the money was gone. In San Francisco a man of Bart's description might walk the streets every day, or come and go as he pleased without arousing the slightest suspicion. But there was little use in hunting for him there. Mustaches and chin whiskers were popular, and there were thousands of elderly gentlemen in San Francisco with the same general description.

During 1881 and '82 Bart held up nine stagecoaches in northern California. Eight of these holdups were made without a hitch. In each of them he slipped from behind a boulder in his flour sack and duster disguise, crouched in front of the lead team with his shotgun aimed at the driver's head, and demanded, "Throw down the box!" None of the treasure boxes had held more than a few hundred dollars, and each had been found at the scene of the holdup, smashed open and with an old ax lying beside it.

The ninth attempt had nearly ended in disaster for the old highwayman. Always before, the lead team of horses had reared and come to a stop when he crouched in front of them. This time they didn't. The frightened leaders swerved aside and raced on, brushing against Bart and knocking him flat at the roadside. He was unhurt, but as the wildly rocking coach lurched away, the driver snatched up his shotgun, turned on the seat, and fired. The shot was a near miss. It ripped off Bart's derby and flour sack disguise, but only one buckshot hit him. It raked a furrow high across the right side of his forehead.

George Hackett, the driver, got only a glance at Bart as he dodged into the bushes. In making his report he said he could almost swear that the highwayman had gray hair and a big white mustache. This was Bart's first failure, and although he had been no more than scratched by the shot, it was a great victory for Wells Fargo. For now Jim Hume had a definite tie between the phantom highwayman and the kindly old gentleman described by Mrs. McCreary's daughter and the Trinity Mountain rancher.

Bart's close call did not seem to have discouraged or frightened him. Two months later he held up a coach running between Redding and Yreka. During

the winter and spring he was back on the coast to
rob the Lakeport–Cloverdale stage twice. By early
summer he had shifted his hunting grounds a hundred
and fifty miles to the southeast, back near the scene
of his first holdup. On June 23 he held up the Ione
stage near Jackson, in Amador County.

For several years Jim Hume had been positive that,
sooner or later, Bart would make a mistake that would
lead quickly to his arrest. Now he believed the time
was close at hand. With each passing year, the number
of stagecoaches carrying Wells Fargo boxes was be-
coming fewer, but Bart had never attempted to hold
up a stage that was not carrying a treasure box. Since
he worked alone it was probable that he spent several
days in a town near which he planned to hold up a
stage, making friends and finding out when a treasure
box was to be shipped.

Following the Ione–Jackson holdup Jim Hume visited both towns, and questioned innkeepers, grocers,
and the local sheriffs. He was not surprised to find that
a kindly old gentleman had stopped at one of the inns
for several days. With two exceptions the description
checked perfectly. One exception was that Bart had
posed as a mineowner, waiting for a friend to join him
before going on to his mine. The other was that the
blanket roll was missing; Bart had carried his belong-
ings in a suitcase.

Until this time all the information Jim Hume and

his men had gathered regarding Black Bart had been carefully guarded in Wells Fargo's vaults at San Fransisco. Hume had not wanted this information to reach the newspapers. Publication would only make the foxy old highwayman more cautious and, if possible, more difficult to catch. But now Jim believed the material should be carefully broadcast. He prepared a four-page circular and had it sent to every Wells Fargo agent, sheriff, and peace officer in the state, instructing them to keep the information confidential.

8

It is said that criminals always return to the scene of their first crime. Black Bart was no exception.

About four months after the Ione–Jackson holdup, Reason McConnell drove his four-horse coach out of Sonora at a fast gallop. With Black Bart having made his last holdup less than forty miles up that same road, McConnell had good reason to hurry. It was still two hours before dawn, and though he carried no passengers the Wells Fargo box held $550 in gold coin and dust worth $65. At Tuttletown, ten miles out of Sonora, he would stop to pick up $4200 in gold amalgam. Worse still, if he should be held up he'd be unable to toss down the treasure box and drive on. Wells Fargo had insisted that on this trip the box be bolted solidly to the floor inside the coach. The sooner that box could be turned over to the agent at Milton, the better McConnell would like it.

Shortly after daylight Reason McConnell pulled his blowing horses to a stop at Grandma Rolleri's little inn at Reynolds Ferry. While he hurried inside for a cup of hot coffee, he left Grandma's nineteen-year-old son Jimmy to watch the coach. As Jimmy stood watching it he decided to ask Reason for a ride over to Copperopolis. That gave him another idea; why not take his rifle along? McConnell would have to let the horses walk on the long climb up Funk's Hill. That would give him time to get down and scout through the brush, then meet Reason again on the far side of the hill. He'd known all fall that there was a herd of fat deer on Funk's Hill; maybe he could get a shot at one of them.

Reason McConnell was glad to have Jimmy's company, and they sat together on the high seat until they reached the foot of Funk's Hill. When the horses slowed to a walk on the first sharp curve, Jimmy jumped down. Slipping four cartridges into the chamber of his rifle, he glided away among the scrub oak as silently as an Indian. By moving right along he could circle around the hill and be back at the road on the far side by the time McConnell got there.

The plodding horses were within less than a hundred yards of the hilltop when McConnell heard a sound in the brush at the roadside. He turned his head quickly and found himself looking down the twin barrels of a sawed-off shotgun. At the far end of them bright eyes shone behind peepholes in a flour sack, and a deep voice asked, "Who was that man — the one who got off down below?"

Reason McConnell caught the note of unsureness in the highwayman's voice, and an idea came quickly to him. "That wasn't no man, but a boy," he answered; "a young fellow from the inn at the ferry. He rode out to fetch in some cattle down yonder that had strayed."

It was evident that Bart believed him, and knew the Wells Fargo box was bolted down inside the coach. Instead of ordering, "Throw down the box!" he demanded, "Throw down your gun and get down!"

As soon as McConnell was down, Bart told him, "Unhook your horses and drive them over the hilltop! Be quick about it!"

McConnell wanted to give Jimmy time to get around the hillside with his rifle. He stalled as much as he dared as he unhitched the horses and drove them out of sight beyond the hilltop. Behind him he heard the sound of heavy pounding, and knew Bart was having no easy time in trying to break open the bolted-down Wells Fargo box.

McConnell had barely driven out of sight from the coach when he saw Jimmy coming toward him through the bushes. He signaled him to be quiet and to hurry. The sound of hammering stopped as they crept cautiously back over the hilltop. At the moment they

came in sight of the coach Bart backed out of the doorway. The flour sack was off his head, and he held it in one hand, partly filled with the gold he had taken from the Wells Fargo box.

McConnell snatched the rifle from Jimmy's hands, jerked it to his shoulder, and fired twice in quick succession. Both shots missed. Bart whirled and ran for the bushes on the downhill side of the road, his derby hat falling from his head as he ran. "Here, let me shoot!" Jimmy shouted. "I'll get him and won't kill him either." He fired just as Bart disappeared into the brush.

It seemed that Jimmy Rolleri was a good prophet.

Bart faltered, looked as if he were going to fall, then slipped away into the thick stand of manzanita. When McConnell and Jimmy reached the spot they were too excited to pick up the fresh trail and follow it. They hitched up the horses, galloped them to Copperopolis, and reported the holdup. The agent there wired immediately to Jim Hume in San Francisco, and to Sheriff Ben Thorn in San Andreas. A posse of townspeople gathered quickly and raced to the scene, each member anxious to have a hand in capturing the famous Black Bart, but even more anxious for a claim to the Wells Fargo reward. In the time it took Sheriff Thorn to ride the twenty miles from San Andreas the posse had managed to obliterate any possible trail, but had failed to find Bart's derby hat which lay right at the roadside.

Ben Thorn was an intelligent and highly observant sheriff. As soon as he reached the scene he took charge of the leaderless posse and organized a systematic search of Funk's Hill. While the posse ranged back and forth through the brush he questioned McConnell for every detail of the holdup and the conversation between himself and Bart. It was clear to him that if the highwayman had been watching the coach as it approached the hill, he could not then have been in his hiding place at the roadside. He would have had to be high on the crest of the hill, and sufficiently elevated to get an unobstructed view across the brush tops.

The sheriff stood for a minute or two studying the hilltop. Near the crest and a hundred yards back from the road, the dome of a great boulder showed just above the ragged fringe of brush. Sheriff Thorn made his way straight to it, and his reasoning proved to be good. This had been Bart's campsite. Behind the boulder Thorn found a case for field glasses, a blanket, belt, magnifying glass, razor, and two flour sacks. In one of the sacks he found three dirty linen cuffs and a handful of buckshot tied up in a handkerchief. He examined the handkerchief carefully. It was of good linen, and carefully marked at one corner in indelible ink, F.X.O.7. In the second flour sack he found two paper bags; the smaller held about a pound of sugar, and the larger was half filled with crackers.

When Sheriff Thorn took the evidence to Wells Fargo's office in San Francisco, Jim Hume was interested only in the handkerchief. He knew the letters F.X.O.7. to be a laundry mark. If, as he had long suspected, Bart lived in San Francisco, this mark should lead quickly and directly to him.

There were ninety-one laundries listed in the San Francisco directory. Jim Hume called in detective Harry Morse, gave him the handkerchief, and told him to check every laundry until he found the one where the mark had been put on. For a week Morse went from laundry to laundry, but the mark was recognized by none of them. With only four left to be checked he hunted out the laundry of Phineas Ferguson on Stevenson Street — hardly more than an alley behind the buildings facing on Market Street. Mr. Ferguson recognized the mark immediately. He looked in his book and told Morse that the handkerchief belonged to a Mr. C. E. Bolton. No, he had never seen Mr. Bolton. His laundry was always sent in by Mr. Ware, who had an agency in his cigar store at 316 Bush Street.

When Morse called at the cigar store, Mr. Ware told him, "Why certainly, I know Mr. Bolton well. He is in the city now; just arrived from his mine two days ago, and if you will call later you will probably meet him here, for he is an old acquaintance of mine and makes this his headquarters when in the city. He lives at the Webb House, a small hotel at 37 Second Street, in room 40."

Morse, of course, did not tell Mr. Ware that he was a detective, but said his name was Hamilton. He spoke as though he were a mining man, anxious to get in touch with Mr. Bolton at once on an important matter. He asked Ware if he would be able to leave his store long enough to take him to Webb House and introduce him. Mr. Ware agreed, and together they started down Bush Street.

They had barely left the store when a dapper, elderly gentleman came walking up the street toward them. He was dressed in a dark suit sprinkled with little flecks of white that resembled snowflakes. He

wore a fine derby hat cocked stylishly on his head. He carried a little walking stick, which gave him even more the appearance of a wealthy man enjoying his declining years, and a diamond pin sparkled from his necktie. As the gentleman came pleasantly toward them Ware said, "Good afternoon, Mr. Bolton. This is Mr. Hamilton who wants to consult you on a mining matter. Now, gentlemen, I will leave you to your business and return to my shop."

Harry Morse suggested that they might go to his office where they could talk more comfortably than on the street. Bart showed no signs of nervousness, but went willingly — down Bush Street to Montgomery, then left to Wells Fargo's building. He made no objection to entering the building and going up to Jim Hume's office, but he became indignant when Jim told him he was suspected of the Funk's Hill holdup. "What!" he said. "Do you take me for a stage robber? I have never harmed anybody in all my life, and this is the first time my character has ever been brought into question!"

Even when confronted with the evidence, Bart would not admit that he had ever held up a stage. Jim Hume was positive of his man. He had no choice but to call the police, have Bart locked up, and secure a search warrant so that his room might be examined. The room held all the evidence necessary for a conviction: laundry bearing the telltale F.X.O.7. mark, the suit Bart had worn when making the holdup, and the linen duster. A partly written letter was found in handwriting like that in a line of verse he had left long ago in a smashed Wells Fargo treasure box. But none of the treasure taken in the Funk's Hill holdup was discovered.

Jim Hume was determined that the treasure should be recovered, but he could find no hatred in his heart for the gentle old rascal who had outwitted him for so many years. If Wells Fargo were to present all its evidence in court, there was no doubt that the old fellow would be sent to the penitentiary for life. If he were to confess the Funk's Hill holdup and return the treasure, it was probable that a judge would be lenient with him.

Hour after hour Hume and Morse talked to Bart, urging him to confess the Funk's Hill holdup and return the treasure. And hour after hour Bart insisted that he didn't have the treasure, that he was a gentleman mineowner and couldn't possibly have been the robber. Then he suddenly turned to Morse and said, "Mind you, I do not admit that I committed this robbery. But what benefit would it be to the man who did do it if he should acknowledge it?"

Again Morse explained to him that if he were convicted of all the Black Bart holdups he would probably go to the penitentiary for the rest of his life. Then he went on to say that if Bart would confess to the Funk's

Hill holdup and return the stolen treasure, or tell where it was hidden, Wells Fargo would not press charges in his other twenty-seven holdups.

"Supposing," Bart asked, "that the man who did commit the robbery should do this, would it not be possible for him to get clear altogether?"

"No," Morse told him, "but it would go much easier for him."

"Well," Bart said, "let's go after it!"

Bart seemed as relieved as Wells Fargo that his career as a highwayman had been brought to a close. He did no brooding about the punishment he was sure to receive, but talked freely as arrangements were being made to take him back to the scene of the holdup. He said it had been his custom to take breakfast every morning — when not away on business — at Pike's on Kearny Street. Pike's was less than a block from the San Francisco police station, and many policemen ate there. When asked if this hadn't worried him, Bart looked surprised and said, "Why no, they didn't know who I was. I never associated with any but good people, and none of them ever dreamed what my business was."

When asked how he was able to get away from the scene of his holdups without leaving a trail, and how he had known when the large shipment of gold amalgam was to be made from Tuttletown, he answered: "Why that's easy. Any man who likes to watch wild creatures has to learn to walk quiet through the woods; it gets to be a habit. It was no trouble to find out when the shipment would be made. I just stopped at Tuttletown for a few days and made friends with the folks who were shipping it. They told me when it was going out and that the box would be bolted down."

Black Bart had become the most famous of all California highwaymen. For eight years the more sensational newspapers had been publishing editorials following each of his holdups, demanding that "this bloodthirsty criminal who is terrorizing the citizens of our fair state be run down and killed, or apprehended and hanged." News of his capture was splashed in headlines from end to end of the state, and sensation-seeking editors clamored for vengeance. The curious gathered in throngs around the San Francisco jail, hoping for a peep at the famous bad man.

Many detectives responsible for the capture of so famous an outlaw would have stepped forward to bask in the limelight and take credit as a hero. And most firms that had been victimized as Black Bart had victimized Wells Fargo would have demanded the maximum penalty under the law. But Wells Fargo was no ordinary firm, and Jim Hume was no ordinary detective. The heyday of stage robberies was passed. They could see no need of making a "horrible example" of this gentle old man in order to discourage others who might be tempted to rob Wells Fargo treasure boxes. Although the cost of trying to capture him had been tremendous, the amount actually stolen in all twenty-seven of his holdups before this last one had amounted to no more than eight or nine thousand dollars. They were interested only in recovering what they could from the Funk's Hill holdup, and putting the old rascal away for a few years so that he could hold up no more stages.

Now that the capture had been made Jim Hume withdrew from the case, and he did his best to protect Bart from those who were howling for vengeance. He was careful that no description of Bart should reach the newspapers, and insisted that he be moved from the San Francisco jail to the scene of his last holdup without publicity. Captain Stone of the police department would take him, without handcuffs, on a river boat to Stockton, and from there to Funk's Hill by special coach. Harry Morse would accompany them, and Sheriff Thorn would meet the boat at Stockton.

In spite of Jim Hume's care, news leaked out in Stockton that Bart would be on the boat, and a crowd of a hundred or more curious were gathered at the wharf. But his identity had been so well concealed that they mistook Harry Morse for the highwayman.

At Funk's Hill Bart led his captors down into a gulch a quarter-mile below the roadway. There he kicked a pile of leaves away from the end of a hollow log, reached in, and pulled out the flour sack he had used as a disguise for the holdup. In it was the treasure he had stolen from the Wells Fargo box. On November 17, two weeks to the day after the holdup, he appeared before a judge of the Superior Court, entered his plea of guilty, waived trial, and asked the court to pronounce judgment. The judge, taking into account that Bart was being accused of only the Funk's Hill robbery, that the amount stolen had been returned, and that in all his long career he had never harmed anyone, set his sentence at six years in the state prison.

Bart was the last of California's famous highwaymen. The era of the stagecoach was drawing toward its close, and with Bart's capture Wells Fargo had carried out in full the policy set down by Henry Wells in its infancy: those who robbed Wells Fargo must be run down and punished. No man had been more responsible for carrying out that policy than James B. Hume. During the years he headed the firm's detective department more than a hundred million dollars' worth of treasure was carried in Wells Fargo treasure boxes. His record, taken from the company's files, speaks for itself:

Number of stage robberies	313
Number of stage robbers killed	16
Number hanged by citizens	7
Number of convictions	240

Treasure stolen
 (all repaid to customers) $415,312.55
Rewards paid 73,451.00
Cost of prosecutions 90,079.00
Salaries of guards and special
 officers 326,417.00

Where other express and stagecoach companies had
been driven out of business by robberies, Wells Fargo
had held its losses to less than one half of 1 per cent
of the treasure carried. For vicious outlaws Wells
Fargo had been unrelenting in its punishment; for
Black Bart, the most famous highwayman in California
history, Wells Fargo had been compassionate.

DURING the years of Black Bart's reign as the Phantom Highwayman tremendous changes were taking place in California. By 1876 the Southern Pacific Railway had extended its lines the entire length of the San Joaquin Valley, over the high Tehachapi Pass at the southern end of the Sierra Nevada Mountains, and into the rapidly growing city of Los Angeles. Other lines of the railroad reached northward from San Francisco Bay through the rich Sacramento Valley, and south-ward through the even richer Santa Clara and Salinas valleys.

Thousands of men who came to California in the gold rush had remained after the placer mines were stripped of their golden treasure. Many of these men were farmers from New England and other eastern regions where the worn-out, rocky soil and cold winters made farming hard and unprofitable. They were quick to recognize the advantages of the winterless climate and the richness of the soil in California's rock-free interior valleys. At the time of the gold discovery these interior valleys were almost uninhabited. Before the railroad had been completed nearly every tillable acre had been homesteaded or bought from the Southern Pacific Railway, to which the United States government had made enormous land grants.

There were only two drawbacks to California farming. One of these was that little or no rain fell from early May until mid-October. With the long, hot summers and the rich soil there was almost no crop that could not be grown if properly irrigated, but without irrigation the land was semi-arid. The other problem was that of marketing the abundant crops that the land was capable of producing.

If the land was well watered, the finest oranges, lemons, figs, and dates could be raised in the southern valleys and on the fringes of the deserts. The Santa Clara Valley produced the nation's earliest and finest strawberries, peaches, apricots, and prunes. During months when much of the United States was covered with ice and snow, the Salinas Valley produced excellent lettuce, celery, and artichokes. Nowhere in the nation could better apples, pears, grapes, and tomatoes be raised than in the San Joaquin, Sacramento, and Sonoma valleys.

But all of these crops were perishable. None of them could be shipped to the ready markets in the East by water. Refrigeration on shipboard was then unknown, and long before vessels made the trip around the tip of South America their perishable cargoes spoiled. Even though a transcontinental railroad had been completed, this was of little help to the California fruit and vegetable growers. A car shipped from Southern California might not reach New York within six weeks. In summer, perishable fruits and vegetables became overheated and spoiled in crossing the deserts. In winter they froze in the slow climbs over the mountains.

As rapidly as railroads were built in the West, Wells Fargo made exclusive contracts with them for carrying its treasure boxes and express on the fastest passenger trains. But as the placer mines became worked out there was less and less gold to be carried, and Wells Fargo needed to find a new source of business. Its far-sighted General Manager, John J. Valentine, realized that the company could grow only if the territory which it served also grew. California was rapidly turning from a mining to an agricultural state. John Valentine reasoned that if Wells Fargo were to prosper, agriculture in California would have to prosper. The greatest needs of the farmers were irrigation and fast transportation of their crops to the eastern markets. Wells Fargo could do nothing about the irrigation problem, and it could not possibly furnish fast transportation for all the perishable crops California was capable of raising. But John Valentine believed there was a way in which the company could be of tremendous help to the farmers.

Because of the mild winters and early springs, California's fruits and berries were the first in the nation to ripen. It was on these out-of-season crops that the California farmers must depend, and it was here that Wells Fargo could be of the greatest help to them. For instance, at the time the eastern strawberry crop was at its height, the berries would sell in New York City at five cents a quart, but the earliest in the market would bring as much as twenty-five cents. The farmers could well afford to pay fair express rates if it were possible for their early crops to reach the eastern markets fast enough to avoid spoilage. And Wells Fargo, with its contracts for having express carried by the fastest passenger trains, was in a position to furnish this service.

There was only one great difficulty: Wells Fargo's contracts with the railroads reached only as far eastward as Salt Lake City. But the Santa Fe Railroad was just completing a direct line from Chicago to California. In order to reach the Chicago markets the firm paid the Santa Fe $1,450,000 for an exclusive express contract. The California market was greatly increased when the Wells Fargo service was extended to Chicago, but this was not enough. If California agriculture was to prosper to the greatest possible extent, the New York market must be reached, and

John Valentine recognized this goal as a responsibility of Wells Fargo. Within a month from the time the Santa Fe Railroad was completed to Chicago, Wells Fargo bought out the Erie Express Company. This gave the firm a direct route from California to New York City, making it the first transcontinental express company in the United States.

With their transportation problem solved, the greatest need of the California farmers became that of irrigation. But this problem they solved for themselves. Banding together they formed water companies, built hundreds of miles of irrigation canals, and dams to store water from melting snow in the mountain canyons. Tens of thousands of additional acres of rich California land were brought into production, the farmers prospered, and Wells Fargo shared in the prosperity.

The route of the Santa Fe Railroad from California to Chicago lay across the hot deserts of Arizona and New Mexico. As the line of rails was extended towns sprang up along it, but there was then no irrigation in this arid region, and no refrigeration. Fresh meat, fruit, and green vegetables for the people of these towns must be brought in by express. But in the intense heat of the summer, the fastest passenger trains were too slow to keep these perishable foods from spoiling before they reached their destination. Here was another problem that needed to be solved quickly, and Wells Fargo solved it completely. The company arranged for the railroad to set aside a baggage car exclusively for express handling, then had large refrigerators built into it.

The car was put into operation between Kansas City, Tucson, and Phoenix. It was a tremendous success from the very first day, and soon the express charges on each trip amounted to nearly a thousand dollars. Wells Fargo ordered more and more of these special cars. But they were very expensive to build, and the railroads could not afford to build them as rapidly as the demand grew. Again Wells Fargo believed it had an obligation to its customers. If the railroads could not afford to build as many refrigerated cars as were needed, Wells Fargo would build them. Before it had caught up with the demand the company had built with its own funds 175 of the finest refrigerated cars in the world. The company's profits boomed, and California became the foremost fruit and vegetable producing state in the Union.

The Wells Fargo banking business was growing as rapidly as the express business. Its headquarters were at San Francisco's Pine and Montgomery streets, in one of the most solidly constructed and finest buildings in the city. The main floor was occupied by the banking room, with a fireproof vault for books and records at the rear. In the basement were the great vaults, believed to be the strongest and safest in the world. Their inner walls were of inch-thick plates of heavy steel. These were surrounded with three-foot walls of solid masonry, and the fireproof doors weighed nearly five tons each. These vaults had been built when San Francisco was "the wickedest city in the world," and it was believed that they had been built so strongly that no disaster could harm them, or an army of desperadoes break into them. On the top floor of the building were the offices, where the books and records of the gigantic company were kept. From the first day of its operation, safety and service had been the watchword of Wells Fargo, and in building its headquarters the firm had spared no expense in safeguarding the property of its depositors and customers.

Shortly before daylight on the morning of April 18, 1906, the peninsula on which San Francisco is built was rocked by a severe earthquake. An earthquake in San Francisco was not unusual, for there is a crack in the earth's surface under the peninsula. But the quake of April 18 was sharp and violent, followed by several afterquakes. A few people were thrown from their beds, many brick chimneys toppled, others were cracked their entire length, some of the poorer business buildings collapsed, but most of the houses and the better-constructed commercial buildings were relatively undamaged.

The people of San Francisco were not panicked by

the earthquake, but it was too near daylight for them to go back to sleep, and the morning was cold and foggy. A little heat would feel good in the house, so they'd have an early breakfast before going out to see how much damage had been done. Fires were started in the cookstoves, the eggs were put on to fry, and many a housewife was annoyed because she had no water for making coffee. Only a drip came from the faucets; evidently a water main had been broken by the earthquake.

In their thoughtlessness the people of San Francisco were destroying their city. As the flames from their breakfast fires were drawn into dozens of cracked chimneys the dry wooden framework surrounding them was kindled. By daylight scores of fires, like a

rash of scarlet fever, spotted almost the entire residential area of the city. With most of the water mains broken by the earthquake, the firemen were helpless. Their only hope was to prevent the fires from spreading from the blocks in which they had started. But the downtown district seemed to be safe. There were no cookstoves there to set the buildings afire, and only a few of the older buildings had collapsed.

The Wells Fargo bank on Montgomery Street opened as usual on the morning of April 18. The great vault doors were swung open and heavy trays of gold and silver coins were carried to the tellers' windows, for San Francisco was the one great city of the world which still refused to use paper money. As the tellers lined up their long rows of twenty-dollar gold pieces in stacks of four hundred dollars each, the bookkeepers took the ponderous ledgers from the record vault, spread them out on their high desks and began their day's work.

In the meantime fires in the residential areas were leaping from block to block as the morning fog was pushed inland by a fresh breeze from the sea. As the sun broke through the fog bank the breeze stiffened, blowing the flames eastward, across Russian Hill, Nob Hill, and toward the downtown district of the city. One pocket of fire spread until it joined another, then still another, until a solid wall of flame swept down Nob Hill toward the financial district. In a desperate effort to stop it, firemen dynamited row upon row of buildings, trying to form a firebreak and save the heart of the city. But with the rising force of the wind it was a hopeless task. By ten-thirty the financial district was doomed. Firemen raced from building to building, ordering all hands to get out before they were trapped.

Frederick Lipman, then president of the Wells Fargo bank, was no man to be thrown into a panic, regardless of the situation. It was evident to him that the city would be entirely destroyed. If a general panic were to be avoided, Wells Fargo must be in a position to pay off its depositors immediately. There was no possibility of removing gold and silver from the building, but this did not worry Mr. Lipman, for the great vaults in the basement were as near fireproof as it was possible to make them. Even though melted by intense heat, the gold and silver on hand would still retain its value, but no bank could keep all its depositors' money on hand. Wells Fargo had loaned three million dollars in New York City. The last telegram sent from San Francisco before the telegraph lines were destroyed was Frederick Lipman's wire to New York, calling these loans and demanding that the money be sent immediately to the San Francisco Mint.

Mr. Lipman's calmness steadied the entire force of employees. Without panic the tellers carried their

trays of gold and silver to the great vaults in the basement. Securities, bonds, and other highly valuable
documents were carried in, and the ponderous doors
closed. The ledgers and records of the accounting
offices were then taken to the vault on the first floor,
but the flames were now dangerously near. There was
now no time for careful arrangement. As fast as the
heavy ledgers could be brought down from the offices
they were piled on the floor of the vault, the doors
slammed shut and the building evacuated.

A few blocks away, over on Folsom Street, Andy
Christeson, manager of the Wells Fargo express business, was showing the same levelheaded coolness that
Frederick Lipman had shown at the bank. Here was
the great downtown express warehouse of the company, and the stables housing three hundred horses
and nearly as many wagons. As the flames raced down
Nob Hill, Andy inspired his expressmen, kept them
from panicking. Every horse was harnessed, every
wagon loaded to the roof, and before the flames had
leaped Market Street — the wide central thorough-
fare of the city — the long Wells Fargo caravan was
racing toward the open fields of Golden Gate Park.
The wagons were no sooner unloaded in the safety of
the park than Andy Christeson turned these vehicles
over to anyone who could save his personal be-
longings. Before the fire had run its course, thousands

of San Franciscans had salvaged enough furniture, with Wells Fargo wagons, to start new homes.

The fire had broken out on Wednesday morning. By nightfall the city lay in ruins and martial law had been declared. On Thursday the downtown district was a holocaust of searing flames and toppling walls. Soldiers guarded the approaches with fixed bayonets, and no citizens were permitted to enter. Frederick Lipman crossed the bay to Oakland where telegraph offices were still in communication with the East. From there he sent wires to New York, London, Paris, and all the important cities of the world, saying: WELLS FARGO BANK BUILDING DESTROYED VAULT INTACT CREDIT UNAFFECTED. He could only hope that the vaults had withstood the catastrophe, but Wells Fargo had become an important force in world banking. Its customers and depositors were scattered all over the globe, and they must be assured that their funds were safe.

On Friday Mr. Lipman was permitted to go to the bank building on Montgomery Street. But the interior of the building had collapsed and flames still smoldered in the ruins. Somewhere under the rubble were the vaults, but there was no possibility of examining them or getting at the treasure they held.

Considering the extent of the fire, the loss of life in San Francisco had been far less than might have been expected, but hundreds of thousands of people had been made homeless. Although the Red Cross and the railroads were rushing in food and clothing, there was immediate need for funds and banking service, and Frederick Lipman determined that Wells Fargo would supply that need.

The western section of the residential district had escaped the fire, and there, in a large house at 2020 Jackson Street, lived E. S. Heller, an assistant teller of the bank. Mr. Lipman went directly from the burned-out bank building to see Heller, and arranged with him to use the ground floor of his house as a temporary bank. Next he went to the old United States Mint on Mission Street, which had miraculously withstood the fire. Of course, there had not been time for funds from the New York loans to reach the Mint, and it had almost no gold reserve on hand, but it did have a large supply of silver quarters. Lipman made arrangements for Wells Fargo to draw against this supply of silver pending the arrival of the gold shipments from the East.

Before the ashes of the destroyed city were cold, Wells Fargo was back in business. The officers of the bank sat around the dining room table in E. S. Heller's home, and here depositors came to withdraw funds and carry on their banking business. There were, of course, no records, and would be none until the rubble could be cleared away and the bank vaults opened, but this did not worry the Wells Fargo officers. They knew and trusted their customers as their customers knew and trusted them. Each man who came to withdraw funds was asked to state the balance of his account, his word was accepted, and he was paid in quarters.

While smoke still rose from the ruins, the businessmen of San Francisco set up temporary offices in tents and shacks, and the rebuilding of the city was begun. The Wells Fargo expressmen were never busier; carrying food and clothing for the homeless, hauling building materials for new construction, and picking up the threads of their disrupted business throughout the state.

Frederick Lipman himself supervised the clearing away of the rubble and the opening of the vaults in the gutted Wells Fargo bank building. The great vaults in the basement had withstood the holocaust perfectly. Its gold and silver treasure was undamaged; the bonds and securities intact. But the record vault on the ground floor had become a bake oven in the intense heat. Record books and files that had been stacked on the floor were baked to flaky ashes, but only one of the banking ledgers had been destroyed. Months were required to reconstruct the records and balance all the accounts, but when the work had been completed Wells Fargo's trust in its customers' honesty proved to be well justified. The loss from overdrafts

was less than two hundred dollars, undoubtedly all due to honest mistakes.

The Wells Fargo banking building at the corner of Pine and Montgomery streets had been so completely destroyed that it could not have been rebuilt within a year. But at the corner of Market Street there was a fine new building that had escaped serious damage. As soon as the new building could be put back into condition Wells Fargo moved its banking business there. Its officers had unbounded confidence in the future of San Francisco, and in its businessmen. These were the men whose enthusiasm and drive had developed San Francisco from a muddy little gold-rush town to a great city. All they needed in order to make it a great city again was financing, and Wells Fargo had the funds with which to do it.

Enormous loans were made with little more security than Wells Fargo's faith in the future of San Francisco and its people, and faith has seldom been more fully justified. Rising like a phoenix from its own ashes, the new city of San Francisco surpassed the old in an incredibly short time. Within months it was again the financial center of the West, and at its heart was the great banking house of Wells Fargo.

As the city and the banking business prospered, the Wells Fargo express business grew and expanded. Day and night its refrigerated express cars sped the most perishable products of West Coast farmers to the markets of the East, and brought back the goods that were badly needed in the rapidly growing West. Its services were expanded from the provinces of Canada to southern Mexico, and prosperity followed in their wake.

To better serve the country in time of war, all the express companies of the nation were consolidated into the American Railway Express during World War I. But Wells Fargo is still one of the best-known and most respected names in California. Each day thousands of Californians come to the Wells Fargo Building at the corner of San Francisco's Market and Montgomery streets to do their banking, and each year Wells Fargo armored trucks carry millions upon millions of dollars' worth of treasure through the streets of the nation's largest cities.

BIBLIOGRAPHY

Autobiography of the West,
   by Oscar Lewis, New York, 1958

Bad Company,
   Joseph Henry Jackson, New York, 1949

The Big Bonanza,
   by Carl Burgess Glasscock, Indianapolis, 1931

The California Earthquake of 1906,
   by David Starr Jordan, San Francisco, 1907

Old Waybills,
   by Alvin Fay Harlow, New York, 1934

On the Trails of Yesterday,
   by Roy W. Cloud, San Francisco, 1931

The Overland Stage to California,
   by F. A. Root and W. E. Connelley, Topeka, 1901

The Pioneer Miner and the Pack Mule Express,
   by Ernest A. Wiltsee, San Francisco, 1931

Six Horses,
   by Capt. William and George Hugh Banning, New
   York, 1930

Treasure Express,
   Neill C. Wilson, New York, 1936

Wells Fargo and Company,
   by Edward Hungerford, New York, 1949

Wells Fargo and Company,
   by Neill C. Wilson, New York, 1936

Wells Fargo and Company,
   by Oscar Osburn Winther, Stanford, Calif., 1936

INDEX

Lightning Source UK Ltd.
Milton Keynes UK
UKHW022114160922
408955UK00017B/466